ENCOUNTERS

PRESSING INTO YOUR ABUNDANT HEAVENLY SUPPLY

By Joshua Marcengill
Edited by Dr. Sherri Lewis

"...It has been written by the prophets, 'They will all be taught by God himself...'"

John 6:45

Copyright © 2019 by Joshua Marcengill

Copyright © 2019 by Joshua Marcengill
All rights reserved. No part of this book may be reproduced or used in any manner without written permission of the copyright owner except for the use of quotations. For more information, email: jmarcengill@gmail.com

Encounters: Pressing into Your Abundant Heavenly Supply

Paperback Print Edition ISBN-13: 978-1-7342850-0-0

eBook ISBN-13: 978-1-7342850-1-7

This book is protected by the copyright laws of the United States of America. This book may not be copied or reprinted for commercial gain or profit. The use of short quotations or occasional page copying for personal or group study is permitted and encouraged. Further permission may be granted upon request.

Scripture quotations used from the Mirror Bible ® Du Toit, Francois. Hermanus, South Africa : Copyright © 2012 Mirror Word Publishing.

Scripture quotations marked TPT are from The Passion Translation®. Copyright © 2017, 2018 by Passion & Fire Ministries, Inc. Used by permission. All rights reserved. www.ThePassionTranslation.com.

Scripture quotations taken from the Amplified® Bible (AMPC), Copyright © 1954, 1958, 1962, 1964, 1965, 1987 by The Lockman Foundation. Used by permission. www.Lockman.org

Scripture quotations marked (NASB) are taken from the New American Standard Bible® (NASB), Copyright © 1960, 1962, 1963, 1968, 1971, 1972, 1973, 1975, 1977, 1995 by The Lockman Foundation. Used by permission. www.Lockman.org

Scripture quotations marked (NIV) are taken from the Holy Bible, New International Version®, NIV®. Copyright © 1973, 1978, 1984, 2011 by Biblica, Inc.™ Used by permission of Zondervan. All rights reserved worldwide. www.zondervan.com The "NIV" and "New International Version" are trademarks registered in the United States Patent and Trademark Office by Biblica, Inc.™

Cover background photo Gatis Marcinkevics on Upsplash

Contents

FOREWORD by Blake Healy   11

Introduction   13

PART 1

What Are Encounters?   23
    Chapter 1 Defining Encounters   25
    Chapter 2 Varieties of Encounters   31

PART 2

The Power of the Testimony   43
    Chapter 3 Do it Again   45

PART 3

Encounters that Made Me a Son   55
    Chapter 4 Encounters from Jesus   57
    Chapter 5 Encounters from Holy Spirit   89
    Chapter 6 Encounters from God   107
    Chapter 7 Encounters from His Kingdom   127
    Chapter 8 Abundance, Encounters and Sonship   141

PART 4

There is Enough   163
    Chapter 9 Repentance is a Lifestyle   165
    Chapter 10 There is Enough   183

Appendix A

How to Tell Your Testimony   209

Invitation   231

Appendix B

365 Encounters Bible Reading Plan   233

Book References   250

Bible References   251

SPECIAL THANKS

There's a lot of people I'll miss here, but I gotta thank my mom who was with me through all the ups and downs. Somehow, she's not mentioned much in this book, but I assure you, she was there. She was there even when I wouldn't let her be there. I'm so grateful for that.

I want to thank my wife, Mary, who seems like the manifestation of a talk I once had with the Lord. He came to me several times, but finally cornered me about it, asking me who my wife could be. All I remember writing down was that she would need to be someone who could always brighten my day. That nothing could steal away her smile for long, even when I was in a dark place. I remember writing that I'd really know she was the one He'd choose for me. And she is, of course, most frequently lighthearted and smiling and there's never been a question about whether or not she was mine or I was hers. His choice helps us choose each other daily. He's a good God.

I want to thank Felipe Muro, my Hispanic dad, who I talk more about in this book. And all of his sweet family who I love forever. The Lord showed me that we'd all have mansions right next to each other in eternity. Felipe's brother, Isaac, who introduced me to a relationship with Jesus and Destiny Church of San Diego with all of my family who I miss daily but never reach out to. It's just too hard to be living in Georgia when I'm always thinking about San Diego.

I'm so grateful forever to Jesse Armas and Jorge Mendez. Grateful to so many others. I'd like to thank Bethel Church for helping me see that I wasn't so different a person alone with my connection to God in the world. I'm grateful to Steve and Lindy Hale, Michael and Kimberly Edwards, Rachel and Kevin Koontz, Jonathan Snyder, Roger Sisk, Charles and Candra Georgi, Zach Aten, Abigail Holt Jennings, Melissa Crilly, Julianne Nolan, Justin and Jenn Stockman, April and Blake Healy and so many others from the Bethel Atlanta community for continually prophesying over me and helping me see that my history with God was valuable and worth writing about for others.

FOREWORD

God's children are designed for relationship with their father. We are built to hunger for His nature, to be drawn in and engaged by the mysteries of His kingdom, and to long for intimacy with Him. We are all born with a fundamental need to be close to Him, a need that is intended to be fulfilled.

Relationship with God is not meant to be an abstract spiritual concept or pleasant religious sentiment, it is meant to be the very foundation of our lives. We have been created to know His voice, recognize the works of His hand, and seek His face. We are designed to have a relationship with Him. A connection as tangible, personal, and affecting as any earthly bond. A relationship that is real.

Encounters invites its readers into a real relationship with God; a God who speaks, a God who guides, a God who loves and loves and then teaches you more about Himself so that you can experience His love more fully.

Here you will find tools to begin building a deeper relationship with your heavenly father, a relationship full of encounters with His presence. You will find testimonies to help broaden your understanding of the myriad ways God is ready to encounter you. And you will find revelations, scriptures, and teachings that reveal a God who has given you His full permission to pursue encounters with Him.

Sometimes; because of our upbringing, church history, or relational patterns; some of us can feel a sense of trepidation when pursuing new levels of intimacy with God. A fear that we are unworthy or unfit to step deeper into His presence. A discomfort at not knowing how to engage with God in a more intimate way. A temptation to take a step back and retreat to the familiarity of distance. If you find yourself having any of these emotions as you take your first few steps into these pages, let me please encourage you to gather yourself, hold on, and take just a few steps closer.

I believe that Joshua has, with this book, released an impartation of the grace on his life for encounters with God. A grace that, I feel, is uniquely suited to helping you be at peace in your Father's presence. A grace that is designed to equip those who have never had a personal encounter with God and invite those who have into a lifestyle of encounter.

Blake K Healy
Director of the Bethel Atlanta School of Supernatural Ministry
Author of The Veil

Introduction

~

Good news!

God. is. real.

He's actually real. He's really real!

And thank God for God.

The following pages were written after many friends and family asked me to write about my *"wild and crazy"* encounters with God. I was persuaded when the Lord told me internally—as clear as you hear yourself reading these sentences—that I could give away what I had received. I guess I didn't like the idea of talking about myself, but I absolutely love the idea of sharing what I've been given! It's simple really, God healed me from the inside out like He does. I want that for everyone. His willingness to do so much for me leads me to believe He is inviting each of us into a level of abundance, through encounters, that the world has never known. It's a glory above yesterday's glory, a heavenly reality here on earth for today. It wouldn't stop Him if we weren't ready for it. He's ready for it, and He decided He wanted us to have this abundant life full of heaven's supply long before we were born.

God is so determined to see us have our inheritance in full that He will even help us to receive encounters abundantly. He'll whet our appetite, teach us to trust Him and bring us full throttle into the deepest, most real moments with Him. I know because He did it for me. He's healed me like only He can do. Way down on the inside where living waters could flow back out. That flow out is the very thing I used to write this book you're reading now.

I stopped many times to restore the flow before completing this project. I wanted to write from encounters about encounters. I can't help but believe He'll bring encounters to you abundantly, moments where you'll know He's real, maybe on deeper, more astounding levels than you have been. Moments that will teach you beyond a shadow of a doubt that you are a son or daughter, an inheritor of Him, the Father, and His abundant Kingdom.

For the sake of your life, of course, but for the sake of the world, too.

What would we do without God?!

Thank God for God.

Thank God that God is real.

I'm aware of the narrative, like a hidden broadcast that continuously plays out there, saying *there isn't enough*. It asks us to tune in daily and would love for us to spend more time confirming its twisted and distorted *facts*. "The end is near; We're killing our planet; We're stealing from our children..." This narrative takes truth and mangles it to serve an evil agenda.

Science isn't our enemy; facts and truth are extremely valuable to all of us, but hopelessness kills, steals and creates fatherlessness in us all. This broadcast has taught these distortions for generations, but God's abundance is about to expose this devious lie so we can see the truth. The truth about the state of our world, the hope we have, and the desperate cry of all creation for the sons and daughters to be revealed.

I got saved when I was twenty-seven years old. God used an encounter to bring me into His Kingdom before I even knew what an encounter was. He has used encounters to make me a son, day after day. A stark contrast to the lifeless, slow death of distorted reality I was experiencing before I knew He was real. I've learned that encounters are a source of discipleship, correction, and love from our abundant Heavenly Father who gives generously. He fills the void we have with more than we need. He fills it with the intention to make it overflow for others. He's generous. Encounters convinced me that He was real. Not facts or persuasive speech, but those overwhelming moments when I had no other reasonable explanation.

Now before we go any further, it's critical for you to understand that encounters are nearly worthless without the spiritual understanding and wisdom that only flows from the Word of God. There's no way around it; we have to get in the Word. I'd hardly speak the language of encounter if I didn't often read the Bible. The Bible is a foundational tool in my walk with God. In fact, in 2009, just two years after I first got saved, God used a random, 365-day Bible reading plan to encounter me each and every day through His scriptures. That's abundance! He was using abundant encounters to both reveal His Word, as well as to transform me from the inside out.

I was becoming so different. I remember when I read bits and pieces of the Bible before I got saved and it always felt dry and boring, but He used encounters to make those same Scriptures real and alive. He brought the characters to life and so much more. I'm thoroughly convinced there is nothing more relevant than the Bible on earth. But we need both the Bible and the reality of God with us for it to not be just another book.

I have also found that we often put up fences, wear unnecessary or unkind lenses and even build psychological walls between us and God, or who He wants to be for us in a given season. God is the same always, but like a good Father, He knows what we need and will provide it, if we don't deny it based on what we think He should or could be doing instead.

While it hasn't been my experience that walls have to be gone before we will receive encounters, I have learned how being vulnerable to God makes life with Him easier to understand. Being vulnerable to God is safer than we can imagine. Having a soft heart, being childlike in our trust and expectation toward the Father, Son and Holy Spirit opens up and creates clarity in our lines of communication as ambassadors and citizens of heaven who live on the earth.

For this reason, I included some powerful prayer tools throughout Part 3 of this book to accompany the breakthroughs and encounters He gave to me, in hopes that I could pass them along. I believe you will find answers that destroy distance and, in its place, build deep connection. My prayer is that these tools help equip you and establish daily fellowship with our living God and His abundance in your life. I pray that you'd be equipped and overflow from the things you've seen Him do in you for the sake of the world.

I believe God is releasing an ecosystem of life and victory that will overwhelm the death, lies, and purposelessness of this fallen world for good. Encounters He gave me showed me His method for doing that from the inside of my heart and through my physical mind. Kindness, hope, and peace were unfolded so that the anxious, depressed crooked places were made straight and lively. If He could do it in me, He can do it for the whole world.

Encounters seem to be a form of currency from heaven that can tip the scales away from the two distracting evils of lack and greed forever. His voice leads me and can lead us all right past all distractions into purpose and destiny. We'll learn to live more like sons and daughters through encounters. Our capacity will expand as well as our sensitivity. The Church will become the spotless Bride of Christ, just like He said in Ephesians.[1]

Some stop believing God for encounters at their salvation experience. Others are still holding on to encounters from long, long ago in a land far away. Some are holding on to their parents', siblings', or friends' encounters. How can we think we won't need and continue to need touches from heaven? Could it be that Heaven throws the biggest party when God's children receive Christ for the first time because they see the connection being established between us? What if their excitement is that it's a ladder from heaven to earth that we just received!

The party doesn't stop if we keep receiving. In fact, to paraphrase from Father Capon, 'it goes from the wine cellar to the main room and takes over the whole house.'[2] It takes over our lives and if we let it, God will use it to heal the whole world. We have evidence; we watched as He did it in us. If He can do it in me, He can do it, period. For anyone, for anything, for homes, for cultures, for business, entertainment, politics, for all the world.

Jesus clearly used daily encounters with God and God isn't holding that back from any of us. Hearing what He is saying, doing

---

[1] *Ephesians 5:25-27*

[2] *Reference from Robert Farrar Capon from his book The Parables of Judgement*

what He is doing – that belongs to us too. Consider it, only an abusive, torturous evil dad would ask us to do "greater things"[3] than Jesus did and then not give us what Jesus had. That's not our Dad. He's a good Father. Sons and daughters know this all the way down. We know we have a right to hear our Father's voice and know Him personally. It is the Christ life available to us because of the price He paid.

He's right here with us now. I pray you can feel Him now, and even begin to experience the excessive, abundant cheering coming from that throne room of angels and the cloud of witnesses. I pray you know, first-hand, why they call it "the great cloud of witnesses!" as you engage with the radical volume of their unhindered cheers! Can you hear their feet dancing? Can you hear their blowhorns and noise makers? That's for you!

"You can do it! He is with you! He's all you need!..."

And increasing now, louder and louder. I ask in Jesus name that God would confirm all this for you before you read another word. I pray His presence would fill you now.

Selah~

(Hebrew for 'pause, breath, and take a second to worship before moving on')

---

[3] *John 14:12-14*

God is not short on encounters, my friends.

PART 1
What Are Encounters?

PART 1: What Are Encounters?

Chapter 1
Defining Encounters

You may wonder how I'm using the word encounter. As of 2019, dictionary.com defines encounter as:

Verb "to come upon or meet with, especially unexpectedly"

Noun
"a meeting with a person or thing, especially a casual, unexpected, or brief meeting"

My attempt at a definition of Encounter for this book's purposes: Individualized experiences gifted by manifestations of both the subjective and objective presence and nature of the living God in our collective natural reality.

Biblical encounters range from Adam meeting with God in the cool of the day to John's accounts of Jesus in the book of Revelation. Enoch walks with God, Mary talks to the angel Gabriel; Paul falls off his high horse on his way to Damascus[4] and so on, throughout the book. Without encounters, the Bible would not have a plot. It's a book of encounter – account after account of God touching man. The Bible is, in fact, a living manuscript and begs to be interacted with. It's not a decoration or a merit to own. The Bible is an invitation to encountering a real God. It's the key to unlocking our hearts to receive from our generous God. That thing we physically receive from Him is encounter.

Christian words like encounter often get thrown around a bit frivolously. It's hard to distinguish *encounter* from the word *presence,* for example. Other terms I hear Christians using to describe encounters include glory, manifestation, revelation, fruit and so on. This isn't a problem for most of us, but for the sake of our journey here, let's look at the contrast between a few of these terms to help pull out and further distinguish our subject of Encounters.

It's very possible that encounters are definitively located snug in between presence and glory. It seems we first learn to abide in His presence—which is, at least at first, an encounter—then, mostly when we are open and willing, we learn to abide in His

---

[4] *Acts 9:3-4*

presence, which produces frequent encounters – moments with God's individual connection and communication to us. Those encounters overflow into genuine glory—the manifestation of heaven on earth. Or sometimes it all happens at once, or backwards. Many have encounters, but don't know the presence and so on. There isn't a formula. There isn't restriction and it isn't something that can be captured by religion and a to-do list. There may be somewhat of a to-don't list, but even that would be violated by its wind-like paths and opportunities it presents. Nevertheless, there at least can be a difference between presence and encounter.

> **Presence** – our acknowledgement of an atmospheric physical reality of the nearness of God. It may be subjective or objective, but it is distinct.
>
> **Encounter** – moments of connection and communication from God.

I also came to the understanding that revelation is not necessarily an encounter all by itself. More often, it is the fruit of encounter. Revelation is frequently the result of our mind participating in receiving an encounter. For example, you may have a moment when you know God is real; that is a revelation that has at emerged above the heart level. That revelation is a fruit of that encounter. To abide there and receive both the revelation and the fruit would be to further press into it to say, "I will never have to wonder if God is real again." Now we have solidified the 18-inch journey from our heart to our head. We just accepted an invitation to live as a son or daughter with a living, Heavenly Father. I've, of course, simplified and generalized an infinitely unique experience with this example, but it might help us grab some common ground and that's the point here.

> **Fruit** – a quantifiable result of an interaction with presence, glory or encounter.
>
> **Revelation** – An understanding our brain or head has consumed/received fruit from our heart after an experience with encounter, presence or glory.

Encounters are face to face moments we share with the Trinity: Jesus, Father God and Holy Spirit; and with heaven: angels, God's constant presence and heaven's higher reality. Glory is the increase of heaven on earth, the manifest establishment of God's Kingdom. For example, if I pray for a person to be healed, I first connect with the love God has revealed to me for that person.

I might receive a Word of Knowledge (something I couldn't have known about them without the help of God, who knows them, telling me). That word then releases revelation (the person realizes that God is real and knows them), which supplies faith and in turn, they get healed by their faith. That person now has heaven's glory. A manifested, objective encounter. A heavenly reality on the earth.

PART 1: *What Are Encounters?*

The fruit of glory now exists, but it's up to them whether they steward it or not.

Glory – When earth is so impacted by heaven that it becomes heavenly, either forcefully or through acceptance and gratitude.

That glory is the presence of Christ in them that is now a demonstration of manifestation that cannot be removed from them. They can forget about it, it happens, but nothing can remove their witness if they decide to have value for that encounter. That demonstration is now a testimony and that testimony of Christ is the hope of all the world. I believe it's even a currency from heaven released on the earth to tip the scales towards abundance. This person's encounter is the very thing that all of creation longs for. The thing the Bible tells us will release all of creation to be like heaven.[5]

---

[5] *Rom 8:18-24*

PART 1: What Are Encounters?

Chapter 2
Varieties of Encounters

It clearly pleases God to give us a variety of encounters, encounters that build trust in us as the individuals He made us to be. He wants us to know that He knows us better than we've ever been known and uses encounters to do that and more. If you've ever received a gift that was really thoughtful, you know what it feels like to get the perfect encounter. God picks the perfect encounter and picks the perfect timing to deliver it. He is the best gift giver there will ever be. Christianity began with a variety of encounters like the ones we'll discuss. Each one was intentionally planned and delivered for the individual person God had fearfully made to receive it.

Encounters are tailored specifically to us for God's purposes on the earth that He has chosen us to achieve or play a role in. Mary, the mother of Jesus, for example, held the word from the angel encounter in her heart[6]. She never would have been the first Christian without that encounter. She was the first to conceive mentally and physically of Christ being alive in her. Wow! Many prophets *per*ceived a savior would come, but Mary *con*ceived the Savior *had* come with the help of her encounter.

Neither can we conceive on our own. We need moments of encounter to conceive, otherwise we perceive, and there is a difference. Perceiving, we may live on the faith of our parents or the people we trust, a book we read, but conceiving means we have internal evidence firmly planted within us. God has given life to a seed within us. God decides what those encounters should be like and clearly considers us as individuals when deciding what kinds of encounters He will give to us. If we value and cherish the unique encounters He chooses for us as Mary did, then we too will see glory manifest from the fertile womb of our hearts.

The following isn't an exhaustive list, but I'd like to describe a few different types of common encounters. We can't limit the God whose thoughts of us are like the sands of all the seas, but let's explore a few common experiences, nevertheless.

---

[6] *Luke 2:19*

Subjective and Objective Encounters

Subjective encounters happen when we are the only observer or witness.

Objective encounters happen when there are multiple witnesses.

Every time a king, prophet, or seer in the Bible hears God, they almost always experience *subjective* encounters. In contrast, Jesus is told He is the Son in whom the Lord is well pleased in front of John the Baptist and the crowds. This was an *objective* experience for all.

It's quite often that I'll hear the same Scripture from my morning reading read from a pulpit, in a movie, spoken by a friend, and so on. This is so rewarding—seeing His hand in my daily moments like that—knowing that God put all the events together that even made my day, seems evident through this moment. It's clear that He builds our days with subjective encounters like these. Encounters that others did not experience in the same way we did, even if we shared them with them verbally. We were there, they were not. These, and other subjective encounters, moments we share with God, are the most abundant encounters available.

If we are awakened to them and value them, we will experience them through every one of our senses, in most of our moments, throughout every day. God is everywhere and in everything all the time. If we have eyes that see, we can tune into that reality anywhere, at any time.

God does speak publicly, but in most cases, it's a closet encounter, a subjective experience we'll have. It is these encounters that teach us about partnership with the Lord, and that's the way He designed it. Just because they are subjective doesn't make them any less valuable.

We are learning to hear through them, practicing our understanding of His leading. I've had subjective encounters that were challenged and even proven to be inaccurate. A word of direction I'd perceive but the end result never connected to the lesson or to the Teacher. I was wrong. No big deal. I'm not sure why I missed it, but I did and that's okay because I was tuning in. Through practice I was cultivating the fruit of connectedness. That's so valuable.

These private experiences can give us confidence that what He did in us, He can do in others. For many of us, we can't imagine

PART 1: What Are Encounters?

Him holding what we've experienced back from others, which can invite us into world-changing zeal. It's why we share the testimony; so God can "do it again." When you've found Christ in you, it actually reveals the hope of Glory for all the Earth. It's what the Bible says the mystery we all want to know is (Colossians 1:27). That's it. It's Christ evidenced in our own reality. We saw Him; we weren't confused. It was as real as gravity. When you know how valuable this is, faith in what you've seen subjectively can bring objective encounters. Those encounters have the power to heal the dying world.

Sometimes, God shows up too and everyone is there to witness it, like glory clouds that have been showing up in church services. Foggy light shows with shimmering gold and silver throughout them. Believe it or not, many people are witnesses to these manifestations.

Miracles like splitting the seas, the ear growing back on the Sanhedrin soldier, Jesus walking through walls in front of the disciples, Peter walking on water, and so many more, are all examples of fully manifested, *objective* encounters. Everyone is a witness. Where things get a little tricky is that every witness has a slightly different experience. Their witness seems subject to their personal relationship with faith and God, perhaps even their value for their own subjective moments with Him.

We get some insight into this phenomenon when Saul had the encounter that resulted in his name changing to Paul on the road to Damascus, some heard a voice there too, others heard lightning, and there were probably some wondering what was going on.[7] This is just like what happened with Jesus when God called Him His son at His baptism.[8] When we've built up our ability to receive encounters from God through expectation, subjective or objective, I propose, we won't be one of those hearing lighting when God speaks; we will be one of those who hear God's voice.

> *"Depths of purpose and layers of meaning saturate everything you do. Such amazing mysteries found within every miracle that nearly everyone seems to miss. Those with no discernment can never really discover the deep and glorious secrets hidden in your ways."*
>
> *Psalms 92:5,6 (TPT, emphasis mine)*

By increasing our value for encounter, we increase our discernment and our ability to receive every type of encounter. It's important that we practice our discernment by activating our expectation. Expectation is just another word for faith.

By keeping our faith on, we will grow in our ability to receive and interpret the constant reality of God alive in our world. What

---

[7] *Acts 9*

[8] *Matthew 3:17*

you witness, you will even be able to help others witness from their own point of view. Your open eyes will help open the eyes of all of God's people. And when a people are ready to believe God for encounter, then walls come down, nations are delivered from evil, and we will see all the realities of heaven manifesting here on the earth.

All my hope is still in Jesus, but Jesus showed me that this is how world-changing occurs. It's only when He saw and heard His Father, who is now also my Father, that Jesus acted. I want to live like that, and God is showing us individually that He is the one who has provided for each of us to do so.

Tangible and Intangible Encounters

Dictonary.com says the word Tangible and Intangible mean:

Tangible - "...capable of being touched; discernible by the touch; material or substantial; real or actual, rather than imaginary or visionary... definite, not vague or elusive... having actual physical existence..."

Intangible - "...incapable of being perceived by the sense of touch, as incorporeal or immaterial things; impalpable... not definite or clear to the mind..."[9]

So many *tangible encounters* have rocked me throughout my life. I've had a comforting hand on my shoulder several times, felt real arms wrap around me for a deeply satisfying hug. I have to assume those were at least angel arms, if not the hands of Jesus Himself. I've fallen down in the natural, slain in the Spirit, but didn't feel a thing, and didn't have a single bruise to show for it. The Holy Spirit would tangibly tickle me in business meetings for a season. I tried to tell Him how inappropriate that seemed to me. Of course, He knew that, but He seemed to have had it with my sullen demeanor. I've had many physical healings in my body. Even healing from the common cold more than once. Apparently, there is a cure. Jesus.

I've even had tangible objective encounters where I felt power come out of my hands when I prayed for people. I'd ask, "Did you feel that?" And they'd respond, "Yes!" And other times, I'd say nothing, but watch as what I felt leave me seemed to clearly enter them. Usually they'd be healed or refreshed, but not always. I can't count how many headaches, backpains and other physical healings

---

[9] *Retrieved on April 22, 2019 from Dictonary.com*

have happened in other people through God using me and moving through me. I can almost always feel Him when He's doing miracles through me, with few exceptions.

Most of the *intangible encounters* I've received have been moments with the word of God. Revelations of truth or connections that I didn't feel like I had a logical origin for but seemed accurate after further inquiry. I remember realizing that Song of Songs was about the church before I read about how theologians had been thinking about this for years. I consider it an encounter because of the deep unexpected connectedness it brought. It also seemed confirmed that it was heavenly truth by the fact that He'd been talking with others about it for so long.

Intangible moments are so pregnant with glory though that they almost never stay intangible. I've had many traumatic memories where Jesus would take me back to them. The memories were not filled with a tangible reality until He brought me back to them. Shame and defeat would do their best to define those moment as they had before, but all of a sudden Jesus is there with me. His tangible presence would instruct and reveal truth that would loosen the grip of shame and guilt and heal an old wound with life and peace. You've probably heard of negative cycles and experienced them, but God has His own cycles that interrupt and obliterate negative cycles. He uses intangible things like honor and kindness to win us over with His love. Love that is almost always tangible but clearly reserves the right to remain hidden.

These moments and moments with revelation all the same tend to result in my most genuine worship as I see His hand. The cycle of intangible becoming tangible is created in this way. My worship focuses His affections on me and often result in more tangible moments from the intangible moments. It seems each of our senses have access to Him tangibly. There is so much that can be cultivated here. Not unlike subjective and objective encounters our value for experiencing these and attributing them to God seem directly correlated to the here-and-now-fellowship with the Trinity they can provide.

PART 2
The Power of the Testimony

Part 2: The Power of the Testimony

Chapter 3
Do it Again

> *...Your miracles have made us who we are.*
>
> *Lord, do it again,*
>
> *And parade from Your temple Your mighty power..."*
>
> *Psalms 68:28-29 emphasis mine*

The Hebrew word "testimony" primarily means to witness or speak of, but at its root, the word can also mean, "do it again." As in, "I'm giving the testimony to give witness to the ability of God to do it again." Consider the use of the verbal history of the Word. Literacy wasn't exactly at a peak in the Old or New Testament days. People in that time told each other stories about God more than they read stories and/or testimonies.

Oral traditions were the Internet of the day, but these were practiced stories. They didn't miss a beat. From fine detail to fine detail, the ancient Hebrews practiced and told the stories under scrutiny of each other for precision. This wasn't a game of telephone, where phrases were lost and added as these stories made their rounds.[10]

For example, they found scrolls from different oral time periods. The documents barely missed a detail from each other.[11] So we know that they must have meticulously kept the verbal accuracy of their stories. That is not easy, but they seemed quite good at it, based on scroll comparison and other archeological finds.

The conversations and storytelling were more culturally significant than they are for most of us today, and for good reason too. Words were seen more like containers than communication. It was and is an art form, right down to the last syllable. During these oral traditions, arguably the most common form of biblical exposure, words carried weight. They must have believed these words were filled with hope and great value; these words were running over with inheritance and promise!

---

[10] *Telephone - the childhood game where everyone shares a phrase in a line by whispering in the ear of the next person. At the end it's far different than the original phrase.*

[11] *A reference to the discovery of the Dead Sea Scrolls. See: https://www.christianitytoday.com/edstetzer/2012/february/closer-look-significance-of-dead-sea-scrolls.html retrieved on 10/26/18*

> "And these words which I command you today shall be in your heart. You shall teach them diligently to your children, and shall talk of them when you sit in your house, when you walk by the way, when you lie down, and when you rise up. You shall bind them as a sign on your hand, and they shall be as frontlets between your eyes."
>
> Deut. 6:6-8 NKJV

What I'm getting at here, however, is the *reason* they told and re-told the testimony – a valuable inheritance for us to consider even today. They told the testimonies to see God do it again and fulfill His promises.[12] And it worked. Joshua repeated one of the greatest miracles God had ever done on the Earth to that day: splitting the Red Sea. Except for Joshua, it was the Jordan that dried up before them.[13]

Later on, Elijah and Elisha split the Jordan together near Jericho.[14] If Joshua could do it, why couldn't they? Wow! These guys were getting excited about what God had done, reminding each other and believing the accounts existed for the purpose that they

---

[12] *Deuteronomy 6*

[13] *Exodus 14:21-31 and Joshua 3:14-17*

[14] *2 Kings 2:7,8 and 14*

could carry them out again! They didn't feel jealous of the testimony but instead, when they heard the testimony, their expectation grew that their God and Father did them for another child and sibling and would surely do it for them as well.

If we ever catch ourselves getting jealous or feeling like God won't do it for us, then we should remind ourselves that we have been adopted into this Kingdom Family. We are heirs to this Kingdom inheritance and where Kingdom demonstrations of the supernatural occur, we receive them into our own account through the gates of gratitude. So many miracles and encounters are extremely personal and individually relevant, but it's the same Spirit that works in us that worked in even Christ Jesus.[15]

There are many other examples of this throughout the Bible. Rocks brought forth water on multiple occasions. Contaminated pools of water and streams, poisoned food, and more were cleaned time and again by those who carried around God-testimonies of old. Oil multiplied, meals were multiplied to feed people in both the Old Testament and the New (check out 2 Kings 4:42-44, where 100 men were fed with just a few barley loaves and ears of corn; and Matt 14:15 and other gospels tell of the fish and loaves that fed 5,000. Gotta love how Jesus escalates things!).

---

[15] *1 Corinthians 12:11*

Part 2: The Power of the Testimony

These testimonies were their treasured inheritance, and now they're yours! This is why I wrote this testimony. I fully believe God will do it again because I have seen it. In the same way Joshua obeyed God and had the men pile up memory stones to help the children of future generations ask expectant questions,[16] this is my testimony, my memory stones piled up, and you now have them in your hand just like Elijah and Elisha.

I believe this book is a container of inheritance, hope, and keys to heavenly storehouses of supplies ready to manifest! It's a promise of what He can and will do for all of His children. A bar raised and a ceiling established, a new standard which I'm happy to see you walk on top of.

Are you with me beloved? Can you perceive it? Share your testimony, share your increase. Share your increase and watch as heaven permeates the earth. He did it in you, and so you now know that He can do it. If you know that, then you have His hope in your heart and the world is waiting for you to know that about yourself. The world is waiting for you to ask our Father to do it again!

---

[16] *Joshua 4*

A Life of Encounters

Moses is a great example in the Scriptures of someone who learned to live out a lifestyle of encounters. If we're intentional as we read through the Biblical accounts of Moses, we can even watch the maturity in Moses as He goes from his life absent of encounters to his life reliant on daily encounters. Moses discovered the reward of a life fixed on the nearness of God. He began to see what His Father in Heaven was doing and hear what He was saying. By that, he found the strength to go from an isolated existence to a lifestyle of leadership and connection to God's presence.

Moses grew an appetite so strong for God's presence and encounter that they became friends.[17] Friendship isn't a one-sided relationship. Friendship is the melding together of hearts. For example, Moses valued his connection with God far above his value to be right about everything. Moses often repented. It was a two-way street, however, as even God repented to Moses.[18] They put their friendship high above their differences and I believe revealed the value of relationship as the best motivation for encounters.

In the following chapters, I'd like to briefly share some of the most significant encounters I've ever had in my life. Encounters that brought me home, gave me a foundation in His word and taught me to live a life higher than my own. A life of friendship with God. These encounters certainty shaped me. They gave me direction and access to my spiritual inheritance in ways I never would have known existed.

As I meditated on these encounters, I picked up on truths, but nearly always long after the time they occurred. Most of these were like puzzles that seemed to be dropped in my lap to figure out. I believe that the process of finding truth is very valuable and so I try to include you in that as authentically as possible. It's like learning to trust that God is always doing something. He's always

---

[17] *Exodus 33:11*

[18] *Exodus 32:14*

got a purpose, within a purpose, within a purpose. It's multilayered truths that when we look, we find more and more.[19]

Above all, I believe in the testimony and its ability to carry heavenly impartation. I believe that testimonies are like the wallets of heaven, carrying around their wealth within. Hearing a testimony gives you permission to receive from the same God who gave it to the person who received it. God is no respecter of persons[20] and so what He has done for me, He will not withhold from anyone else. So, take what you need or what you want. Believe God for the breakthrough. I am praying that God would use my words as containers of His love, healing and any of His provision for your life.

The chapters are broken up into a few of my most significant encounter testimonies. I begin with my Jesus open vision encounter, then my Holy Spirit baptism, Dinner with Father God, Church as a Family and finally, the 365 Encounters that God used to make me a son and teach me to steward my inheritance.

Meeting Jesus set me free from anxiety and purposelessness. Meeting the Holy Spirit put life in me from above. Meeting God made me a beloved son, and finding a church family gave me a home. It was the year of 365 encounters that taught me to live in the house with God. Something that is available to all who are

---

[19] *Proverbs 25:2*

[20] *Romans 2:11-16*

on the property of God. Prodigal Sons like me, older brothers, field hands and even loving fathers (this reference to the parable from Luke 14 is further explored in the next chapter). We all eat from His table together and so here is the place where no matter who we are our paths do intersect. All of these encounters I share have brought me into a sort of sustainable state of internal revival that I believe God wants the whole church to have. I know that I can't do that, but He can, and I've witnessed it happen within myself and even move from me to some others. I pray everyone will know Him, that the whole of creation would know the joys of adoption into the Kingdom of our God and know His personal connection to each of us. I'm here to tell the testimony!

PART 3
Encounters that Made Me a Son

Part 3: Encounters that Made Me a Son

Chapter 4
Encounters from Jesus

Luke 15

The Prodigal Son from Luke 15 is often very much like the testimony that many of us have. We were lost ourselves, or we were out in the field ourselves, or we would have given anything to have someone lost come home. There're so many testimony-like stories in this one parable. Each character and even the scene are dripping with redemption. I can look at this story through different characters' eyes or *lenses*. There's the father lens, the son's lens, the prodigal's lens, the religious lens and so on. So much of my growth and experience with Jesus has revolved around this story from Luke 15, in fact, that I decided to help refresh our memory of it and begin with it here:

> *Once there was a father with two sons. The younger son came to his father and said, "Father, don't you think it's*

time to give me the share of your estate that belongs to me?" So the father went ahead and distributed among the two sons their inheritance. Shortly afterward, the younger son packed up all his belongings and traveled off to see the world. He journeyed to a far-off land where he soon wasted all he was given in a binge of extravagant and reckless living.

With everything spent and nothing left, he grew hungry, for there was a severe famine in that land. So he begged a farmer in that country to hire him. The farmer hired him and sent him out to feed the pigs. The son was so famished, he was willing to even eat the slop given to the pigs, because no one would feed him a thing.

Humiliated, the son finally realized what he was doing and he thought, 'There are many workers at my father's house who have all the food they want with plenty to spare. They lack nothing. Why am I here dying of hunger, feeding these pigs and eating their slop? I want to go back home to my father's house, and I'll say to him, "Father, I was wrong. I have sinned against you. I'll never be worthy to be called your son. Please, Father, just treat me like one of your employees."'

So the young son set off for home. From a long distance away, his father saw him coming, dressed as a beggar, and great compassion swelled up in his heart for his son who was returning home. So the father raced out to meet him.

> *He swept him up in his arms, hugged him dearly, and kissed him over and over with tender love.*
>
> *Then the son said, "Father, I was wrong. I have sinned against you. I could never deserve to be called your son. Just let me be—"*
>
> *The father interrupted and said, "Son, you're home now!"*
>
> *Turning to his servants, the father said, "Quick, bring me the best robe, my very own robe, and I will place it on his shoulders. Bring the ring, the seal of sonship, and I will put it on his finger. And bring out the best shoes you can find for my son. Let's prepare a great feast and celebrate. For this beloved son of mine was once dead, but now he's alive again. Once he was lost, but now he is found!" And everyone celebrated with overflowing joy. (Luke 15:11-24 TPT)*

My prepared speech was a little different than the Prodigal's from this parable, but I can definitely relate to the pig slop, as that felt like all life had to offer me. I felt left out of the party in life and sometimes even worse, like it wasn't a party and anyone who thought otherwise was deceived or faking it. I was stuck here somehow, against my will, scrounging for what scraps I could find. I couldn't imagine hell being any worse.

For me, I hadn't started walking toward my Father's house until 2007 but, like the Prodigal Son, I had a speech prepared whether He would listen or not. I wasn't even sure He was real. But I called out to him one night. I told Him, "You can have me if you want me. If not though, please, just kill me." Then I got really serious and said, "I'd prefer hell to life so get on with it, if that's all there is." If He wasn't real, I knew nothing mattered and I was speaking to the air. If He was real, I had decided that I didn't deserve Him. What got me so low? How did I go so prodigal, so outside of my Father's estate?

Part 3: Encounters that Made Me a Son

There's Not Enough for Me

Growing up, my family never settled for long enough to put down roots in extended family or community much. As a result, we were more like a family of friends. My brother and I were like little adults. Short of the Lego toys we played with near constantly, we hardly spent our youth as kids with parents. We didn't have a lot of kid friends and we didn't do many kid things. Don't get me wrong, my mom and dad were wonderful parents, but the difficulties of life and poverty had brought them to their knees about eighty percent of the time. My brother and I were commonly brought to the table as we faced the many difficult decisions and challenges we had as a family.

I don't know if you've ever visited a poorer country and realized that wealth doesn't truly come from money. You look on the faces of the truly impoverished and you quickly discover joy and lightheartedness in those places of extreme poverty. But for us, it felt like money was always the issue. I remember feeling pretty shocked the first time I had this realization as I visited Peru and was invited into huts where they'd give me a steak that cost them a month's wages just because they were so honored to have me. I wish I could have learned this truth sooner in life, but North American culture seems to be very often poor when there is no money. That's all it takes for us to feel miserable, even worthless. My family's poverty, at least, was caused by a lack of money. I mean we had each other, and we even lived at the beach, but we were weighed down with generational guilt and shame.

Not having money always had us feeling left out and victimized too. We had a lot to handle that was very real. Our mindsets weren't helping though. Life didn't feel light; it felt very unfair and impossible. Between the real tragedies we faced and the mindsets we approached tragedy with, we seemed to enter into a downward spiral pretty early on in my life. It's all I knew.

Most likely, we started downward around the time my dad got sick. I was just three years old when my dad received a diagnosis of HIV. It was the eighties, before anyone knew much about it, so we all assumed my dad would die any minute. The doctors weren't much help at bringing hope either because they didn't seem to know much. The whole HIV thing was new then and people were scared, accusatory and mean to our family upon finding out. It was a family secret because of that. Another block between us and real relationship with others. We kept our guard.

Shortly after the diagnosis, my grandmother and aunt were in a tragic accident where a man running from the law ran a red-light and killed them both. My dad never fully recovered from feeling the weight of this loss and his illness. He would eventually take his life. For all the years in between he fought rejection, depression and heaviness. Pain beyond anything I could imagine. Ironically to all of us, after all this time, the HIV didn't come close to killing him, he had a normal T-cell count. No, it was clear that it was the emotional weight of it that did him in. It was the looming threat of pain and death that proved too much. I was fifteen by the time he'd killed himself.

We were mostly ready for it, having had the threat for over a decade. Still, my dad was my best friend, and all this loss was heavy for all of us. For an introvert child and then adolescent like me, it was a lot to overcome. Too much.

My mom, on the opposite side of the spectrum, was the light in our family's darkness. She was and is one of the most loving and forgiving people I've ever known to this day. Whatever we lacked in money and joy, we did have in love, thanks to her. A true librarian-type, red headed introvert, she was the stabilizer when life got to be too much again and again. A glue holding us together. She cried here and there, but we knew she was tough. She was so tough, I remember one day she turned yellow and green like an unripe banana and fell to the ground after finishing the dishes. Kidney failure. We never would have known. She may have seemed tired that day, but not life-threateningly tired. We were shocked.

This was just before my dad passed, adding to the weight of this seeming ongoing downward cycle. My mom did recover and went on dialysis for a number of years. She continued to be the light and would eventually receive a transplant that she still has.

As you could probably imagine, I wasn't doing so great around all of this. I was making some of the worst decisions of my life already. Wanting to be more like my dad, I had been smoking his cigarettes for a few years at this point, without my parents or anyone else knowing. I know now it was an attempt to self-medicate, as I was already plagued with suicidal thoughts and anxiety from the time I was maybe nine.

Drugs and alcohol weren't at all hard to find in the little beach town where we lived. I started with the typical gateway drugs like marijuana. I didn't know it then, but in addition to self-medicating, I was looking for identity in all the wrong places. Amongst other personalities I tried on, one of the most dangerous was drug dealer.

During this time of my life, I attempted suicide more than once and kept trying out different varieties of identities to see if any of them would fill the emptiness I felt or bring some sort of power into what felt like such a victimized life. This went on for several years and no identity ever really seemed to help. Of course, all I ever tried was bad guy identities – punk, headbanger, mean Irish drunkard, and so on. I eventually decided I wanted to try being a good person, but even that would end up feeling empty to me. Luckily, it wasn't as destructive as the other ones, and it stuck for quite some time.

Part 3: Encounters that Made Me a Son

For me, being a good person didn't mean going to church. I need to back up in my story again to explain, but my mom had taken us to church when I was younger. Somehow, I never heard good news there. I only remember hearing that I was a sinner and that I'd go to hell because of it. That can't be all they talked about, but that's all I heard. My mom gave me a choice when I was about ten and, of course, I didn't want to hear any more of that, if for no other reason than to avoid the added anxiety it brought. I opted out of church from there on. No, being a good person, for me, meant I wanted life to not be so hard for everyone else like it was for me. I was going to fix the *not enough*.

It was noble; it was a new identity. I distinctly remember the course change. Maybe because it was one of the first times someone besides my mom ever seemed to actually believe in me. It was my boss at a video store I worked at. He asked me one day, "Why don't you go to college?" I was shocked that he thought I even could. So, I went.

I'm so grateful to that man; Kevin was his name. Even though I didn't get saved, or find what I was looking for, it was a real turning point for me, a curve in the cycle. A curve that eventually helped break it too, but unfortunately for me I still had a few tragedies to get through before that.

About the time I started college, my brother committed suicide. We hadn't been friends since I was about thirteen, but that didn't mean this was something I was used to and could easily digest. It was a girl. He had met a girl who toyed with him too much. We could never make sense of it.

There was a silver lining as that morning, he told me he loved me as I left for work at the video store. I wonder if it was Jesus because Jimmy, my brother, never said such things. It meant the world to me. He shot himself later that day with a gun we didn't even know he had. It was hard for me, of course, but I was consumed with concern for my mom. How my mom made it, I'll never know.

I felt overwhelmed by seeing my mother break down, knowing I'd need to be there for her more than I ever had. I couldn't do it. I had struggled with drug addiction since my dad's passing and for a while, alcohol took over. I kept it together in front of my mom, but I felt like I was going to have to make some major changes somehow, only I didn't have the strength to do it alone.

The Lord came out to help me. Breaks down my theology in ways, but seems He doesn't care much for the rules when they get in the way of Him and His kids. I had a flash there on the couch on the day of the suicide. It was an encounter sure enough, and one He gave to comfort me, no doubt. Not the first encounter I'd ever had and I'm not sure what I called it then, but I know now it was one for certain. God's unoffended love for me didn't mind that I didn't know Him. He saw a prodigal child in need and did what not even the father from the Luke 15 parable could do. He came out into my prodigal world after me.

The vision was like a TV screen that took over my sight in a moment of subjective encounter. For about thirty seconds to a full

Part 3: Encounters that Made Me a Son

minute, I saw memories in front of me of every good thing I had ever shared with my brother. The times we laughed together or played and loved each other. The encounter caused me to burst into hard tears for maybe thirty minutes and afterwards, I felt more able to help my mom and be there for her thanks to the wealth that encounter brought with it.

My mom and I were all there were left of our little family of four. The two of us adapted like people do in tragedy. No one really knows how you do that, but the fact remains, for saved or unsaved, that God is with us and has made us to overcome. I hadn't lost my pull to get my life together, if anything I felt more conviction that I was on the right track. No one, including my friends were making it out of the life we were living healthy. Many died early tragic deaths. We'd lost count. I was still dealing with suicidal thoughts daily, and a couple of days without a high of any kind felt really hard, but I was up and trying almost daily. I had a purpose. It was finite but it was enough to keep me going passed others who dropped like flies on my right and on my left.

It was a shocker to everyone, especially me, but I was good at school. At first it was really hard, but I wanted it bad enough that I changed the way I managed my life to achieve there. As I went to school, I dreamed of a day when my life wouldn't be marked by poverty. That was the dream. Academically, I fell in love with sociology. I felt like the world's problems weren't unlike my own. I saw a macro to micro picture in that. The world seemed to be dealing with depression just like I was and so all my micro psychological problems seemed to be evident in the macro world. A world in psychological turmoil. I could relate to that. I wanted to stand up for the world that couldn't stand up for itself. So close but so far away from truth.

As I finished up my undergraduate degree, I still felt pretty unsafe financially and so I got an MIBA, a Masters in International Business Administration. At this point, I fully wanted to help the world, to be a good person, and I thought I could do it through business as much as anywhere else. Additionally, I believed that business would secure my freedom from poverty.

In sociology, the topic of Economies of Scale had come up. Economies of scale basically means when companies have so much money that if they make a decision, the world economy feels it. I figured if I could influence *economies of scale* to help alleviate poverty, then the world could be a better place. I went after it and even got a job at one of the world's biggest leadership organizations at the time. I worked in the custom consulting department and we had million-dollar contracts with all the very biggest names in business. I was on my way to be the best person I could be. Truly good, I thought. I was achieving my *good person* dream.

My plan was to graduate and write a book based on my well-researched approach to *giving in order to receive*. It even sounds kind of Christian, but I had worked out the math is all. If I could help companies give in order to receive, then I believed everyone would win and poverty would be destroyed for all people. It was pretty lofty, but I was all in, working eighty hours a week. I was so committed, but it was more than I could handle, and the bottom eventually fell out. Being a good person still wasn't enough.

My First Life-Altering Encounter

Back at my apartment, with my prepared speech like the Prodigal Son, I let a 5th of whiskey put me to sleep on the floor. Remember, I told the Lord if He was real He should kill me and so I genuinely hoped I'd never wake up, but I did. To this day, I still wonder if, in fact, He actually did kill me. No doubt about it, I woke up to a new life that morning, just a few hours after I'd passed out. I don't know about the son from Luke 15 and how he reacted to the party he was brought into, but it would take me some time to catch on. All I knew was that it all just felt so good suddenly. I also knew that it shouldn't. I should have had a painful hangover from the whiskey. It felt undeserved to say the least, but it also felt different from any day I'd ever had.

I felt so good I went for a jog and the atmosphere was new. It was early and there weren't many people around. The air was filled with moisture as if a rain cloud had touched the ground. It was a majestic morning in San Diego, California where I lived at the time, sun piercing through the fog and moisture with countless light rays and rainbows everywhere. It all felt so alive with contrasting tones and abundant peacefulness.

As I jogged that morning through one of the most beautiful parks in the world, Balboa Park, I had an encounter. It was a clear open vision, but not like the memory vision I was given when my brother died. I looked off into the natural horizon. As if from nowhere, I saw black creatures. They appeared fixed, but surrounded me in the distance. I realized they were countless demons, demons resembling the orcs from Lord of the Rings even, except fully dark like charcoal. They kept their distance as I ran, but I suddenly noticed them inching closer.

Even with fear creeping in, I rationalized what I was seeing. I had never seen such a thing, and even though it didn't feel as scary as it looked, it was certainty bizarre.

My friend, Blake Healy, author of *The Veil* and Director of Bethel Atlanta School of Supernatural Ministry, sees in the spirit. His life is like an open vision of sorts. He describes seeing in the spirit like looking through the windshield of a car. "You can focus on the windshield, but if you focus on the road, it's almost like the windshield isn't there."

I felt like I could focus on what I was seeing in the spirit but if I wanted to, I could defocus all the same and just look right through it. I could choose to see them, or not to see them. My hunger for spiritual realities was newly in the driver's seat, so I pushed into it rather than pulling back.

As I continued to jog, I suddenly remembered a statement I had made when my brother committed suicide years earlier. I had said it under my breath, "Any demons that were there to torture my brother, I want you to come to me now and not go into the world. Come to me instead."

This theology was Hollywood-driven, I suspect, as I've always loved watching movies. I wanted to protect the world from what had happened to him. My heart was in the right place, but of course, those demons honored this request. These seemed to be them, in fact. Maybe they added a few buddies too.

I was still jogging. Just when I was about to ignore the whole encounter and try to defocus from the windshield, so to speak, a jogger ran up next to me. I wasn't sure if he was in the natural or spiritual realm. I politely ignored him until he began speaking to me. It was Paul from the Bible.

My mind just knew who Paul was without him telling me. My mind was fruitful I guess, like it had arrived in a place that was already prepared for it. He was dressed in what looked like the typical biblical attire to some degree. He was a Jewish man who'd lost most of his hair on top, but wore modern glasses that probably didn't exist in his day. He didn't smile much, but was very calm and looked very intelligent. I'd love to remember what he talked about. I'm sure it was valuable, but somehow, I wasn't ready to digest it. In my defense, I had no idea what was happening.

Eventually, Paul turned onto a side path. I remember more about Peter than any one I met on that jog. Peter, too, was Jewish, tall and really funny. I remember he was wearing big tennis shoes and his knees came up real high as he ran. He made me laugh out loud, which wasn't something I did back then. I was such a stoic person with my MIBA and my important job. I thought it was my whole worth.

Peter also had ideas.

"You see those demons?" he asked. Believe it or not I had nearly forgotten they were there with everything else going on.

"You can kill them off!"

"How?!" I asked.

"How? Any way you want to! In fact, if you want, you can invent weapons like in a video game. Try it!"

So, I did. I hadn't played video games in so long, the only ones I could remember were like Sonic the Hedgehog. I struggled trying to think of myself as a weapon like Sonic, curling up in a ball. Finally, I decided I would hit them with a whip as they ran at me, and as I did, they shattered like black glass into millions of pieces. I never broke my stride. I just kept jogging.

Next, I shattered them with a sword, sometimes a whole group of them at once. They looked so big and gnarly, but they were deceptively defenseless. Even when I thought they were taking a swing at me, nothing they did ever connected.

Once the sword grew heavy, I tried a few different guns. I suddenly realized I must look like a total weirdo since I was making the motions in the natural world as I attacked the demons in the spiritual. That self-conscious thought gave me an idea.

If I can make up anything, I can make a sonic boom release from my foot every time I hit the ground! I'll take them out by the thousands, I thought. I really just wanted to keep myself from further embarrassment if people in the park saw me making motions and all like some crazy guy.

Peter and I were having a great time, but somewhere along the way I lost him, but the demons kept coming. They were getting closer and breaking through my defenses after a short time.

Just when it got a little too intense, Jesus jogged up in front of me. He looked back at me and I was shocked at the kindness in his eyes. I always thought He was judgmental. That kindness was so deep, I realized I'd never seen it before. This went far beyond any kindness I had ever experienced. When He spoke, He used my first name but omitted the "ua". It was so casual, a nickname—like I was family.

"Josh," he said. "Would you like me to take it from here?"

I thought about it, and with a sense of false humility said, "Nah, that's okay, I can do it. I think I want to."

I gave him a half smile. Thinking back, I can't believe I said that to Jesus! It makes me give a kind of nervous laugh to this day.

I just didn't get it. This was Jesus! But He didn't appear to be even slightly offended. I just watched as He jogged ahead over a hill.

I looked beyond Him and saw a massive dragon with at least three heads. It was waiting, raging over the hill. I kept running and killing the demons. I was getting tired when I had a seemingly random thought and remembered the flood from the story of Noah. I thought, if God could flood the earth, then maybe He could flood the spiritual world I was seeing here.

I asked, "God, could you flood these demons?" and I watched as pools of water that looked like oceans formed below me. The waters rose quickly, and I took a deep breath as they went over my head. I felt like I might drown, but then it rose far over me into the sky. I breathed out with a burst. Unaffected and relieved, I watched as the demons all floated upward, dead from the weight of the violent oceans God had unleashed. They were floating up for miles in the distance up into the sky. I knew at that point I never could have killed them all. I was overwhelmed by how incapable I was, and surprised that I seemed invited to even try.

Learning to Rely on Christ for My Breakthrough

> *"So God created man in His own image; in the image of God He created him..."* Gen. 1:27 NKJV emphasis added

> *"But we all, with unveiled face, beholding as in a mirror the glory of the Lord, are being transformed into the same image from glory to glory...."* 2 Cor. 3:18 NKJV emphasis added

> *"... Those who make [idol images] become like them, so do all who trust in them!"* Psalms 135:18 NIV emphasis added

> *"For as he thinketh in his heart, so is he..."* Prov. 23:7 KJV

Part 3: Encounters that Made Me a Son

Getting a chance to see my enemies' image with my eyes was more valuable than I could have imagined. I saw them, and I remember what I saw. Much later, I realized that I learned a lot of things by looking at them and even learned to defeat them by seeing both them and seeing Jesus. Seeing them in the light of the image of Christ, I knew that what they were was what I had been becoming. I had not been becoming Christ, but rather becoming less and less like Jesus it seemed clear now.

Seeing this contrast equipped me to choose. Let me explain. I had been facing overwhelming anxiety, hopelessness and depression. These things were scary and intimidating, and I assumed I could not overcome them. When I saw these creatures or demons with my eyes, however, I eventually recognized them to be those very things I was feeling, spiritualized. Or perhaps those things, anxiety, hopelessness and depression, were spiritual but had become naturalized in my mind. They had manifested in my natural reality.

To be fair, I wasn't all the way made in the enemy's image. I had hopes to defeat poverty and live a better life, but even that felt like a constant nagging pain because of their incessant torture. I was bankrupt of all gratitude. Wiped out of every ounce of it by the mindset I had throughout my youth and adulthood.

The truth these demons worked so hard to conceal from me was also their biggest fear for themselves. By seeing them with my eyes, I didn't know it yet, but it was exposing the weakness of my assumptions about their strength against me in my life. By seeing

Christ and beholding the kindness in His eyes, I was learning that my assumptions had created a distorted reality for me. My heart was filled with gratitude for the fact that Jesus was actually real.

> *"Then the serpent said to the woman, "You will not surely die. For God knows that in the day you eat of it your eyes will be opened, and you will be like God, knowing good and evil." Gen 3:4-5 NKJV*

I did not need to eat their fruit in order to become like a god. I was already made in the one true God's image. They used intimidation to make me feel like I was overwhelmed and alone when I, like Eve, was already made in the image of God. I gave in to their subhuman idea of what my life could look like. Apparently, my mindset was like a seed I was planting, tending, and keeping in my heart and the fruit that was sprouting up was all my hopelessness, anxiety and depression.

Their seeds of the knowledge of good and evil was the establishment of fallenness in my life's image. It's nothing new. The same lie they've been telling all my ancestors before me and at least for these demons it was simply my turn to receive their doctrine of defeat. As I received their incessant ideas about hope and life and came into agreement with it, I became it.

As I gazed on the contradicting kindness I saw in the eyes of Jesus, I was lifted up and their evil schemes were exposed. I was also equipped with His image, which allowed me to see how silly anxiety, hopelessness and depression truly are. Like little dogs with big barks. The truth was even more deep, as these little dogs weren't making my identity; they were un-making it.

Through the Psalms, we watch as David picks up on this and uses the truth to put some scoffers in their place, "*Scoff at every scoffer and cause them all to be utter failures! Let them be ashamed and horrified over their complete defeat.*"[21] I'm not the failure. I'm not the one that is ashamed or defeated, they are! It's *their* turn to be the anxious, depressed and hopeless ones.

As I am delivered, they are brought into deeper bondage. My enemies are not people or other religions or any such flesh and blood, but they are these spiritual powers and authorities telling me who I am and wanting me to believe in their scoffs. These are the enemies of my soul that would have me defeated in constant anxiety, but Jesus leads me into His kindness and gratitude for His kindness is the identity my heart is healed by when it produces its fruit of kindness. Jesus is like the tree of life,[22] but at a minimum, the better image seed made for my heart.

I did learn to let Jesus take the fight, but it took time, years even. Even today, they do their best to have a platform in my heart.

---

[21] *Psalms 70:3 TPT*

[22] *Prov 13:12, Rev. 22:2*

They work to tell me things like how I can have more anointing or more something else. Don't let anything talk you into using your own anointing when Jesus has given you His. Jesus is all we need. He's not cleaning our filthy rags so we can use them once again. He's replaced them already and we're being given the understanding. We need to be free from the bondage that we still need to earn something. We need to receive Jesus. With eyes on Him, lack and every unrighteous thing is exposed as small and easily overcome. He earned it all for us already and He's given it to us now.

It felt good to see my enemies defeated, but revenge isn't mine in that I don't execute it or carry a single concern about it. That isn't for me either. Revenge is the Lord's and He will have His day of enthusiastic rage against all the enemies of the Kingdom and its fullness.

Belonging to God, I know He is my defender and woe to those silly powers and authorities that came up against His image in me. They didn't come up against me, they came up against Him. I mean, eek, I wouldn't want to be them. I've had a taste of anxiety in this life, like a bite of hell on earth, but they'll *become* anxiety for all of eternity. One day, we'll all forget about anxiety forever. The angels will ask us how God brought us out during the time of our deliverance and we'll just point to Jesus. "He gave His Son so we could be sons and daughters," we'll say.

Our lives are not about defeating the enemy. Our lives are about living from victory, the image of Christ risen with the keys to death, hell, and the grave. If we spend our time on earth fighting, then we miss out on the life and victory we've been given.

No, what I gaze upon I will become, and I am gazing on Christ who Himself is God, made in the image of man, made in the image of God. Jesus Christ made a way for me to connect to Father God, the one who knows me, and the only one who can tell me who He created me to be. He's where I get my image from. Jesus established my eternal identity and I'm looking on to become it. It's not about the fight I was in. It's about the kindness in His eyes, the joy He had as He looked at me, someone He clearly loved. I still have a lot to learn but this, this is a big deal.

Becoming Breakthrough for Others

What I've seen Him do in me, He will do in others. This allows me to come to the table He's prepared for each of us and get equipped for the sake of others. If someone comes to me with a story about hopelessness, I know a few things about what they might be dealing with. Yes, they will have their very own list of *truths* they're believing. But those *truths* may be simple lies I can see through. If I can help them see the capital 'T' Truth, then I can help them manifest their true image. I know that hopelessness is not their portion. You see "...the testimony of Jesus is the spirit of prophecy."[23] and so I have something to say. Having encountered Jesus like this, I have been equipped with the gift of prophecy, and that is a gift that God gives to empower us to set His children free.

---

[23] *Rev 19:10 NKJV*

When it comes to prophecy, I know that their future has hope (see Jeremiah 29:11 for that Truth in the Bible). If I can help them see that, then I know that what I am giving them the opportunity to do is receive life. I'm giving them seeds that can bring forth a harvest of good fruit in their life. I'm also doing my best to expose the hopeless devils as the ones destined for hopelessness. I'm handing that back to them and helping the person embrace the victory of Jesus in their life.

This is also true for the culture I am a part of. If I know that Jesus is the hope of life for myself, then I know that He is the hope of life for humanity. If my culture is dealing with depression or anxiety, then I know that Christ is the solution for these things as well. Micro versus Macro again. All my micro breakthroughs have macro power to set the nations free, in fact.

I know what hopelessness, anxiety and depression truly are and I know how fragile they are. They do their best to intimidate, but the image they portray is easily destroyed by the access that Jesus gave us. Peter told me that any weapon I could imagine would destroy them and I watched them shatter like glass. I was fully persuaded by this encounter God gave me.

Knowing that God can do it in me is knowing that He can do it period. I know something about who God is now. God is the one who defends us and saves our lives. In the same way that He flooded those demonic forces that had overwhelmed me, He can do that for the culture. Like me, the culture may need to see the contrast

I saw, but if I am that contrast, then I am a part of a very powerful solution.

Part 3: Encounters that Made Me a Son

Prayer Activation

Take a moment with each of the following exercise questions, prayers and activities. Give yourself a minimum of 3-5 minutes to respond to each.

Most of the following tools are adapted from the Sozo Ministries' inner healing tools. You can find out more about Sozo online at www.bethelsozo.com or look for a sozo counselor in your area to help facilitate these, and similar prayers and activations. I do recommend that you look for official Bethel Sozo counselors who are certified to use Bethel training tools. You'll find them on that website. If at any time during these prayers and activations, you feel like you're stuck or it's not working, then I'd recommend visiting your local certified Bethel Sozo counselor.

When I say Jesus, what do you see, sense, or feel? Write it down.

_____

_____

_____

Did you have any trouble seeing or experiencing Jesus? If so, ask Him why. Say, "Jesus why can't I see you?" and write that down, whatever He tells you. If instead of seeing him, it's a person's face you see, ask Jesus if you need to forgive that person. If it's a wall, ask Him if He wants to help you take it down. Keep asking questions until you hear from Jesus. You have the right to hear from Jesus. You are a Christian and His sheep hear His voice. Keep asking and believing.

_____

_____

_____

Part 3: Encounters that Made Me a Son

Do this next step after making that connection. Even if you're not sure it's real yet. If it is you'll know. Ask Him now, "Jesus, what do you think about me?" Write down what He tells you.

_____

_____

If you feel like hopelessness, depression, anxiety or any such things have manifested in your image, ask Him what you are believing that is a lie. "Jesus, am I believing any lies about myself or about you?"

_____

_____

If you heard a lie, be sure to ask Jesus what the truth is and write that down. Do this a few times if needed. Get it all out so you can be sure you're believing truth.

_____

_____

_____

Did you have an encounter during this exercise? Or do you want to read about other encounters that people have had? Visit our Facebook group to tell others about it and spread the good news. See Appendix A of this book for help writing or filming your testimony. I believe God wants to normalize the supernatural lifestyle of encounters daily and the thought of having a database of the supernatural activities of God thrills me to no end. I pray that you receive these encounter gifts abundantly. Please see Appendix A for more information.

Part 3: Encounters that Made Me a Son

Chapter 5
Encounters from Holy Spirit

In Over My Head Testimony

I'm skipping ahead a bit in my life story. Skipping past my baptism in Christ, some hardships and life changes, but this book is more about my encounters than about me. I had a crazy encounter in late 2008 that left me with a new gift to speak in tongues and the tangible indwelling of the Holy Spirit. This encounter took away all my ability to control my life. I felt mentally, emotionally, physically over my head during it and learned to live life that way more often from it. I was out of my control and into His control and it was the most radical encounter I had ever had.

Near the Christmas season of 2008, an opportunity arose for me to travel to La Paz, Baja Mexico where a sleepy little town needed help raising awareness for a new church. We came with financial support and big plans for a Christmas festival that would help a new church gain momentum with the locals. I was invited near the last minute, but I jumped at the chance to see what God had for me there. I was passionate about helping out, of course, but it was like I knew something big was there for me.

On the first night we arrived, the group I was with and I attended a service at the church, but it was in Spanish. No translator, so I was lost for the most part. I figured I'd stay to be supportive. Everyone we had traveled with was there, maybe fifteen or so of us. As I sat in the back, a friend translated some of the message to me. Near the end of the message, the passion intensified and despite the lack of translation, I was connecting to the emotion in the room.

Suddenly, I was interrupted by what I felt like was water at my ankles. The church was still under construction, so I looked down, wondering if a new pipe had been put in wrong and burst to flood the place. No water. No one else was reacting to water either. I was startled that I was in the midst of what must be a really tangible encounter. This spiritual water kept rising to my knees and waist and I could feel it the whole time physically. It came up to my neck and I felt fear as my head went under. Right around this moment, my friend who helped translate some of the message leaned over and said, "You should go up. He's making an altar call!"

At this point, I was feeling what can only be described as intoxicated by the overwhelming presence of God. It was a Holy Spirit baptism, but He was just getting started. I stumbled forward,

Part 3: Encounters that Made Me a Son

pushing plastic chairs from one side to the other. I got to the front and to my surprise, there was an English-speaking man, "Pastor Tom," who came to pray for me. He knew exactly what was happening to me, it seemed. As he approached me, he put his hand over my heart without touching my chest. He said, "Son, you need to turn off the analytics here."

He nailed it because my mind was desperately looking for a footing, anything to grab a hold of. I calmed my mind at his request and the next thing he said was, "Open your mouth and make noises." He read some Scriptures from Ephesians 6:19 and Acts 2:4 to help me see that the apostles first opened their mouths before they were given utterance (given the gift of tongues).

All I know is that worked and as I opened my mouth to begin, I vocalized a bit, but then out came the sounds like a river. I was distracted by Pastor Tom's hand, which seemed to be an uncapped, spiritual fire hydrant, and the intensity kept increasing. I had to look to see if he was touching me, but his hand wasn't even on my chest. It was four or five inches away. Fresh clean water that I could physically feel, penetrated my chest from his hand and shot right through me! It took a ninety degree turn at my heart and came straight up and out of the crown of my head! Bursting out!

This was not a vision. It was physically felt, but clearly not actually happening in the natural. It was at that moment that my mouth was going so fast with sounds and utterance that I couldn't stop. At this point my feet felt like they had left the ground. I'm not sure when or how it ended. I was like a drunk man, not even remembering how I got home.

Waking up the next day in my bed, I knew nothing would ever be the same. Being that I am an analytical person, my second thought was to wonder if I could still speak in tongues. I'd heard of the gift, but never wanted it for myself. It had always felt a bit confusing to me. I didn't condemn it, as the Bible says not to, but I didn't see how it would ever come into my life. Turns out that's just the way God wanted it for me.

For whatever reason, I didn't try it out again until that night. I think it was because so many people were around me during our stay there. We were all staying together in the same room and driving around together, so I was rarely by myself. I was shy about it and still thought it was weird. Honestly, I still do, but I'm not ashamed of it as I was then.

I had to work through it, but not at any expense to my relationship with God. On the contrary, He was there, giddy, giggly and joyful the whole time. People were excited to ask me about it too because they saw it happen at the church that night. I tried to brush it all off in an effort to compose myself. That feeling in my chest had hardly left though, and I felt like I could cry at a moment's notice. My whole life felt so much lighter and more beautiful. That night, as I found some privacy, I gave it a shot and there it was. I could barely turn it off. So much! As if it were backed up inside me, waiting to be released.

Just then, to my great joy, I recognized what I was saying! My analytical mind was being satisfied as my "knower" seemed to know what I was saying. I thought a lot of myself. *Not only can I pray in tongues, but I can interpret my own tongues!* I was so encouraged! It was all so real.

Holy Spirit had taken all the guesswork out of it. Only I wish I had known there was some strange time limit on it. Exactly at the two-week mark, my interpretation of my own tongues seemed to shut off. I could still speak in tongues, but it was as if the Holy Spirit wanted to show me they were real, so He gave me that gift to see it for myself. I am able to interpret my own tongues here and there, but for the most part it was a very special time. This encounter, like most encounters had a massive upgrade to bring into my life. The time of interpretation He gave me sealed the gift in me for good.

Learning to Be Supernatural

There is a difference between having the Holy Spirit visit you or come upon you and having Him come to live on the inside of you. Many talk about this better than I will here. Bill Johnson and Graham Cooke are some of my favorite teachers on this subject. Bill talks about the dove who comes to rest on you for the sake of others and in you for your sake. Graham talks about the *habitation culture* of the New Testament, versus the *visitation culture* of the Old Testament. These are just some of my favorites, however.

Most seem to point toward Kenneth Hagin and some others when it comes to the subject and I believe they have a lot to offer as well. Still, nothing beats a real relationship with Holy Spirit to help you sort out the truths you wish to be established on.

I had many moments of visitation after my salvation. I remember walking into a bar and feeling out of place. People began coming to me who I didn't even know to tell me that they didn't think I should be there. There was also the way I quit smoking cigarettes. I forgot to smoke for three full days. For anyone who has smoked, they know how impossible that would be. I had tried to quit many times without success. But there I was in a grocery store practicing my normal routine. I asked the guy behind the counter if I could get a pack of smokes and, WHAM! All at once I remembered that I hadn't smoked in three days. I looked at the man for a full fifteen seconds before I could answer and looking at the pack of cigarettes, I told him, "Never mind, I think I'll pass this time." I never smoked another cigarette.

As I mentioned, there were other occasions I believe the Holy Spirit came upon me, even before I got saved, but having Him in me was different. He made me feel powerful and courageous. I did things I never thought possible, like preaching, laying hands on the sick and more.

Bill Johnson talks about how the Holy Spirit will still visit you when you have Him in you for the sake of others and so that does seem to be a thing in my case as well. He still visits me for the sake of others, but He also moves through me to others when I pray. That courage He brings by being my trusted Friend and Confidant is the strength He's given me to be a world changer.

Apparently, the Holy Spirit is in wild intercession for us. He is praying fervently for each and every one of us. He is praying, Jesus is praying; it's all happening. Jesus made a way to Heaven so I could know the Father. Holy Spirit gives me physical access to heaven and what is pouring out on the earth. He is the conduit that effectively makes me a vessel of heaven walking the earth. He invites me to play a role in what He is doing.

My interpretation gift gave me some insight that may or may not be relevant for others. I know it was helpful to me, but God can do whatever He wants with this gift, whenever and however He wants to. I certainly don't feel like an authority on speaking in tongues.

The brain takes in billions of bits of information every second, but only presents a few thousand to us I believe. But with tongues, I felt like my prayers had access to all of it somehow, and I could process stuff from my memory that I didn't even remember seeing. If my consciousness were an iceberg as is commonly illustrated in psychology, then these spirit-filled prayers seemed to go well below the surface of the floating iceberg to reveal the massive depths of ice mountain below that actually allow the tip to be seen from the surface.

My prayers were rarely, if ever, self-focused. They were mostly about someone else. With the subconscious also engaged, I picked up wild details about their life that seemed easy to identify. I'd imagine that if I were suddenly able to access my entire subconscious naturally, it would take time to figure it out, and learn how to decipher, but it was all there already as if I was an old pro. My mind was fruitful as if a bud suddenly opened up to receive the sunlight.

For example, in less than a second's time, I'd see the lines in someone's face and it would remind me of a point in my life that would somehow show me some current pain they were experiencing. I'd pray for them specifically based on this information. It all lined up as if the veil I'd always been shrouded under had been removed and there I was watching the "magic" happen as all the gears turned right in front of me. I was so amazed at how real it all was. It wasn't magic. It was reality.

> *"...and it was ankle-deep... and it was knee-deep... and it was waist-deep... and it was a river that I could not pass through, for the water had risen... a river that could not be passed through..." Ezekiel 47 (selections from verses 3-6)*

When we consider depth, it's easy to think about deep dark isolated oceans, but clearly God is leading us deeper for something we can be a part of. For Him, depths are places where the limits of our humanness meet with the connection to His deity. He leads us into the deep so we can begin to see how we rely on Him, and so we can do greater things with Him. Way over my head, I was able to rest in His gifts and they brought me closer.

He entrusted me with gifts so He could provide a way out. I didn't know it, but I had constructed a sort of prison in the shallows, utilizing all of my analytical gifts to support it. As I gave over my analytical gift to the Holy Spirit, He didn't remove the gift but gave it back to me without the cage I'd created from it.

I was free to move past the depths that I thought I was keeping myself safe from. He called me into the deep, out into the unknown, so that I could be even closer to Him. It is in Him that I have my being and nothing He is inviting me to is without value. I can trust Him.

I pray in tongues often and I believe that even when I'm not moving my lips, I'm in continued prayer. This gift is not something I claim to understand, but I am fully convinced of its significance to my depth in God. Among many other things, it is access to His deepest places. Many miracles have occurred out of this place of dependence.

He brought His supply through His Holy Spirit and handed over His storehouse keys to me. With my access keys, I have more than enough trust to give away that tongues are real and important to God. It's as if He carved out a place for me to understand something my own natural mind couldn't accept. This felt and feels like a massive spiritual promotion and I believe it has brought down my own strongholds of limitations I had held up to keep depth out. This is what an increase in freedom feels like! Where the Spirit of the Lord is, there is freedom.

Part 3: Encounters that Made Me a Son

Becoming Supernatural for Others

There's no getting around it, the Holy Spirit is here to seek and save the lost. He wants blind eyes open, deaf ears hearing, crippled walking and demonized people free and alive. He is life and life more abundantly and He wants us all to have all that Jesus paid for. He is not afraid to raise the dead and bust up a funeral or booze up a dry wedding even. He is love and purity and while He doesn't check with me about my reservations as often as I'd like, He is also a gentleman and very willing to sit back and let me learn.

I've even stepped into services where I didn't feel Him on me and asked where He was. He said, "I'm an inconvenience here." He always is what we need, whether we think so or not. I'm sad that we sometimes put things above Him, but I have faith that like He does for me, He will reveal our strengths and weaknesses in time. He loves our help and support, but He doesn't need our permission to effect change.

His perspective is infinite, and He offers it to us. There is simply no one we can trust more, but He does seem to expect us to believe that about Him. He wants us to be brave and passionate for the sake of the world, to give up our hopeless worldviews entirely. He is a flame of fire upon us and a cool stream within us. He's in us for us and upon us for them. He takes people to mission fields, movie sets, political office and so much more.

He is the companion all of us need as well as the one that will give us the right words to say when a moment can pivot the future. The Holy Spirit gives gifts and courage to nations and will empower the people to become the church rather than the church to stay a building.

When the one billion soul harvest that many have prophesied for the past thirty or so years comes, there won't be enough churches on the planet to hold the harvest of souls. The ones with the Holy Spirit will be the tabernacles needed to help bring in the many who will be in need of a church. For many, we might be the only Bible they ever see or read, but when they look in our eyes and see the light of the Holy Spirit, they will be ignited to burn as well. We'll see.

Jesus sat down when His work was finished, but He sent us the Holy Spirit to help us do it from here. Without the Holy Spirit, there is no real power. He is the one that brings true authority. Where power corrupts the human heart, He is always pointing to Jesus so that our hearts stay protected. We can literally do all things with the Holy Spirit. He is the gift of God in us, the manifestation of

Part 3: Encounters that Made Me a Son

the Spirit and attitude of Jesus from the inside of us. He teaches us to become like Jesus and supplies access to heavenly gifts that make it so.

Prayer Activation

Take a moment with each of the following exercise questions, prayers and activities. Give yourself a minimum of 3-5 minutes to respond to each.

Just like before, the following tools are adapted from the Sozo Ministries inner healing tools.

When I say Holy Spirit, what do you see, sense, or feel? Write it down. How can you describe the Holy Spirit that you are experiencing? Many have trouble with this one, likely because there aren't many depictions of the Holy Spirit, but trust that He is here and helping you, even protecting you.

_____

_____

_____

Part 3: Encounters that Made Me a Son

Was it too hard to see or feel the Holy Spirit? If so, ask Him why. Say, "Holy Spirit why can't I see you?" and write that down, whatever He tells you. If it's a person's face you see instead of the Holy Spirit, ask Holy Spirit if you need to forgive that person. If it's a wall, ask Him if He wants to help you take it down and then take it down with Him. Let Him walk you through the whole thing using the imagination He created in you. Believe me, Holy Spirit can sanctify our imaginations for His purposes. We hand it over to Him when we believe He will do it. The point is to keep asking questions until you hear from the Holy Spirit and feel connected.

_____

_____

_____

Do this next step after making that connection. Even if you're not sure it's real yet. If it is you'll know. Ask Him, "Holy Spirit, what do you think about me?" Write down what He tells you about you.

_____

_____

_____

If you feel like you need to maintain control, or that you may have misunderstood or overanalyzed the Holy Spirit or any such things have stuck out, ask Him what you are believing that is a lie. "Holy Spirit, am I believing any lies about you, or about myself?"

_____

_____

_____

If you heard a lie, be sure to ask Holy Spirit what the truth is and write that down. Do this a few times if needed. Get it all out so you can be sure you're believing truth.

_____

_____

_____

Did you have an encounter during this exercise? Or do you want to read about other encounters that people have had. Visit our Facebook group to tell others about it and spread the good news. See Appendix A of this book for help writing or filming your testimony. I believe that God wants to normalize the supernatural lifestyle of encounters daily and the thought of having a database of the supernatural activities of God thrills me to no end. I pray that you

Part 3: Encounters that Made Me a Son

receive these encounter gifts abundantly. Please see Appendix A for more information.

Part 3: Encounters that Made Me a Son

Chapter 6
Encounters from God

Dinner with God

Things got pretty tough in my life, after I received the gift of praying in tongues. I was on a spiritual high, but almost simultaneously my life got harder than it ever had been. We completely lost a nonprofit business that had been going really well. I thought that business was my whole Christian future laid out before me, but instead it came to an abrupt and unjust end. I was so confused. Things I thought I understood about being blessed and the love of God felt like fairy tales. Rejection, a common theme in my before-Christ life, seemed to reemerge as the total victor.

I lost everything financially, doing what I could to hold onto hope with my credit cards. To make matters worse, I broke my arm and suddenly had a need to take painkillers. Even with Holy Spirit there, having been addicted to opiates for years, I didn't want to open up that door again and I was scared. Exhausted with rejection and overwhelmed with every detail of reality, I wanted to die again. There wasn't a chance I wanted to return to the life I knew before Christ, but I couldn't see a way forward either. It was another kind of overwhelming pressure.

Just before I broke my arm, I had found out I couldn't pay my rent and would need to sell all of my stuff and potentially live homeless. A coworker from the nonprofit asked me to move in with him when he found out I was going to lose my apartment. I didn't expect that. He was a friend, but he was a Hispanic man with a large family. He was reaching out to me – a strange white guy with no family around – and he wouldn't take no for an answer.

Despite all of that, I had received so much rejection at this point that his acceptance didn't count for much. I even reasoned he was doing it out of penance or something. I took him up on it though. What choice did I have? I gave his family everything I owned, but what he would give me was more generosity than I could have ever imagined.

My arm was broken by the time he took me in. He invited me into his three-bedroom home and showed me to my own room. His whole family—three young kids, two teens, and wife—would all sleep in the other two rooms. He invited me into his family.

Before we go further, I have to back up to tell a little side story. God had been asking me to buy this book I kept seeing called, *The Love Dare*. At the time, the movie, *Fireproof*, had just come out, and somehow this book that was associated with the movie appeared everywhere I went. In the movie, the main character uses this same real book to "fireproof" his marriage. I remember seeing the movie and book in rental stores, in Christian bookstores in the big display; even in the 7/11.

It was a 40-day devotional for married couples to help them restore their marriage. I was so confused why God seemed to bring my attention to it so frequently. I thought, 'What am I going to do with this?' After some time, I decided to give them away to married couples, like "you're welcome," to appease that still small voice. I had to keep buying this book every time I saw it. It felt like a little side ministry I had.

I gave one to my friend who took me in, just a few months before moving into his home. And back to the testimony, there I was, in my own room in my friend's house, on painkillers, deep underneath the full weight of rejection in every aspect of my life. Head hanging low, I shuffled into the bathroom in the middle of the hall and there on the back of the commode, was that book! *The Love Dare 40-day Devotional.*

I couldn't believe it. I was annoyed at God, like, "Why do you keep putting this book in front of me?!" As I asked Him, I opened the book and realized it was actually about restoring relationships between people that love each other and have committed to a covenant. A lightbulb came on. I realized God was inviting me to a 40-day devotional that would restore our covenant relationship together. Hope poured into my heart, enough to wake me up.

I read that devotional every day along with my Bible reading in the morning. Without a job, I dove all in to fasting and meditation. But priority number one was that devotional. I met Him each day in those readings. I devoured that book. Any Scripture it provided I studied. The concepts were like life to me. I repented when it said to do so. I gave myself over to it because the nearness of God was my reward it seemed.

The book was incredibly healing. God had to teach me a different way of being, of living my life before I would ever feel accepted again. Between this book and my 365 day Bible reading plan, this began the year of encounters that I'll talk about in Chapter 8.

On roughly day nineteen of *The Love Dare* devotional, it says to take your spouse to dinner. Anywhere the book said spouse, I put Father God in its place. I didn't think too much about this one at the time, so I just had dinner and thought about what it would be like to sit with Father God for maybe thirty seconds. I got distracted by the food. I thought, "There. I took God to dinner. Great. Done. Check." And I went on about my night.

Fast forward to day forty and I had completed the entire devotional. Around 11pm that night, my life changed again forever. I was driving and stopped at a stop light. Just then, out of nowhere (or maybe "out of everywhere"), I heard the audible voice of the Lord!

"I want to eat here."

Part 3: Encounters that Made Me a Son

His voice was so full and loud, the windshield glass should have busted, but it didn't. It was like nothing I had ever heard. I knew exactly where He wanted to eat as I looked diagonally across the intersection. It was an Asian fusion fast food restaurant. I was a little surprised but obeyed, mainly out of fear.

I pulled into the parking lot, took a deep breath, and moved quickly. I went up to order, but the man stopped me, "Sir, I'm sorry but we close at eleven."

All the rejection I had ever felt in my life immediately hit me like a flood. I could have collapsed, but somehow, I didn't. I genuinely thought I had lost my mind. I thought, "I'm hearing voices and it's all over now. I've been having open visions, speaking in tongues. I'm going to end up in a mental hospital!"

Before I got too far along in that thought, that same man stopped me on my way out. "Sir, sir!" he said, "It's okay sir, you can eat here." He must have seen my dejected shuffle toward the door. He continued, "If you don't mind, I just cleaned the dining area and I will keep the lights low so that no one else comes in."

Life rushed back into me, but before I could get too excited, I realized I was about to eat a meal with the God of the universe. The weight of rejection was fully displaced by the weight of Holiness! I was going to order food for God! Whoa.

What do you order from an Asian fusion fast food restaurant for God?! I had no idea, and I couldn't understand why I picked what I did. I just decided to order God a kid's meal. All I know is that I was overthinking everything! I decided to only get one drink so the man wouldn't think I was bringing in someone else. After I finished, he produced the meals quickly on a tray. There was a drink, one adult meal for me, and one kid's meal for God. Yep.

I was beginning to feel overwhelmed by His thick presence too as I gathered my napkins. I decided to get two straws for my drink in case God wanted some. I didn't know what to expect. I went into the dining room and sat down. As I did, His tangible presence covered me from head to toe. I looked around and realized I was in a pristinely clean environment. The guy might have used a buffer in there because everything was shimmering. The lights were low and from the sound system in the store, I realized I was listening to some seriously cheesy love songs from the 70's. Lyrics like "I will love you forever" and "my love will never die." I took a deep breath, breathed out slowly taking it all in. I realized,

'God. is. *romancing*. me!'

It was so pure and holy. I was a man being romanced. I began to eat. I wondered what would happen to the kid's meal. I had placed it across from me, and I thought *Maybe it'll combust in a fire ball from heaven.*

When that didn't happen and I was wondering what to do with it, I heard a still small voice in my head say, *"Remember the priest."*

Part 3: Encounters that Made Me a Son

And just then I remembered how the priest in the Bible would eat the sacrificial offerings, and how the New Testament called me a priest. I got a little religious and ate every last piece of rice out of those two containers.

Leif Hetland, a missionary to the Muslim world and a friend from my church, would have called it a "baptism of love."[24] That's exactly what it felt like. I had been baptized in water with Jesus, in Spirit with the Holy Spirit and now in love with Father God. I didn't create any doctrine from these experiences; it's just what happened.

I don't remember leaving or going home. I don't remember the Lord saying anything else to me. He didn't have anything to say against me, however. And that was lifechanging in the same way that Jesus' eyes being kind was. There were no "if" statements, like "If you could just change this..." or "If you'll do this for me..." None of that. I couldn't stop reflecting over and over on what He didn't say until I realized that all I felt was the deepest love. It was unconditional love. I realized that this time I was in over my head in love. I was dipped so far down into the love of the Father.

That was the meal He wanted to eat with me. Rather, the meal He served me. As I ate with God, He fed me the most healing, unconditional love you could imagine. He just loved me because He loved me. It wasn't anything I had done or didn't do. He romanced

---

[24] *Baptism of Love book by Leif Hetland*

me because He loved me and wanted me to feel it and know it to be the pure truth. It became a foundation for me. It became the ground that any seed would have to grow on in my life because it was more real than anything I'd known. God loves me.

Rejection didn't stand a chance. Loneliness and hopelessness have not been able to take root because of this one meal I had with God. They were ready to devour me when the man asked me to leave the restaurant. I don't know why that guy turned around to invite me in. What I do know is that I feasted on God's unconditional love right there in front of my enemies. I saw them cast aside, so insignificant. I saw their true form, so small, so powerless. I quickly forgot they were there. Looking back, I know they were there so that I could see them in the light of His love. I could see there's no competition between good and evil, right and wrong; there is only life. God is a Father who wants His sons and daughters to come home to the table of life.

Part 3: Encounters that Made Me a Son

Learning to be Loved

All along in my journey, God has taught me how He needs my whole heart. I even wonder if He gave me a new one just so that I could receive from His. To be loved by God, I need do nothing, as His love is already abundantly flowing toward me, but if I want to be aware of it, then I cannot afford an ounce of hardness in my heart. God speaks to my heart and the minute it isn't soft because of a financial difficulty I'm struggling with or because I've become offended, I've closed my son ears and put walls between me and my Father. These things build walls, and while God will speak to me despite all of this, I may not realize that I'm no longer listening to Him.

We're not on the same wavelength. I've begun, what I like to call, a dirge. A dirge is basically a cryptic, dark melody full of sadness, deep anguish and/or angst. God might sing a dirge to get on my level, but this isn't on His personal playlist. He's the God of life, not death and a dirge is a sad song full of darkness.

It's not like we need to change the dirge. As I said, He'll sing it with you. Many times we sing a dirge in the midst of mourning our losses and nowhere in God's heart is He offended by our mourning. David often sang dirges throughout the Psalms and God faithfully met him there to collect His tears. It's a sad song, but God is not in a hurry to change it. Sad is an emotion He created. The dirge is coming from our heart and God is not working on our thoughts, he's healing our hearts. He's always way down on the inside. If you can't find Him, you're the one putting yourself away from Him. He didn't put you away. We are the ones taking thoughts captive to hand over to Christ, but not Him. We're practicing purity because He is pure. We find something that's not right, we pluck it out and walls removed, relationship restored.

So what makes our hearts hard? Unforgiveness is probably number one, but there is the hardness of life and toil, as well as other things. Our hearts seem to defend themselves if we suffer, leave them unprotected, abused, mistreated, undervalued, despised and so on. We might have been attacked, or we might be the ones attacking ourselves. Our hearts, made to be like gardens of vibrant life, become instead a dry arid land; desertification has removed our hearts ability to even drink in the rain when it comes. Sometimes the desertified heart even becomes so dry, cracked and hard that a rain will cause a destructive flood, rather than healing and nourishment.

In the actual deserts of the earth, scientists have revealed that the ground goes dry when salt light and water stop communicating with each other. I'm simplifying it, but that's really all it is (sodium, chloride, phosphorus, hydrogen, oxygen and so on stop working together to create ecosystems that support life). Not unlike what happens in our hearts. Our heads reason away our feelings or push down and oppress our joy as inappropriate. The lack of communication somehow puts a halt to communion. It pushes out the rains when they come. We might even get offended as it rains, creating more damage.

Restoration begins as we begin to look for ways that God is providing and creating a conversation. God is speaking, and we, through humility and gratitude have complete access to join the conversation. Our communion with *salt, light* and *water* bring in a true relief. A stream comes gushing in and the garden of our hearts begin to reemerge with the promise of fruit to come. Hope is restored.

The Love Dare 40-Day Devotional somehow helped me to discover the communication problems I was having in my heart. My dry desert-like heart was invited into the restoration process. At this point, I even wonder if it's a lie that we need desert seasons to grow at all. I've told my heart to forsake the desert season theology. If we've had one, we've had too many. It's time for some *dessert seasons* instead!

Forgive as quickly as an offense comes! Believe as quickly as a doubt appears. Sing the songs of joy in the darkest of holes that you may find. How? Trust and raise the value we have for hearing His voice. He is speaking, supplying the rain. If we aren't hearing, it's not a sin, but it is a tragedy. By not hearing, we could be causing great damage as well. We need Him. His voice is the most valuable aspect of our lives. In the same way that a desert cannot heal without a communion of elements, we cannot truly experience wholeness without our Father.

He is worthy of our ears and our trust. If we must reason, then reason how worthless it is not to trust Him. If He is not our defender, then what hope would we have? But we do have hope. If there is a break down in communion, then find your heart and break it free from its cage with forgiveness or hope. Let the cool refreshing rain soak into its soil and trust that process. Your heart was made to know God's heart and to walk around in it, discovering new rooms made and prepared for only you!

God is love. Be loved, because you are the beloved. Be loved and communication will flood your world from the throne room. You will see the Defender, Father God at once to subdue your true enemies. The Advocate, Jesus will speak out in front of others of your true worth. The Comforter will bring you an embrace full of truth of purpose for going forward. You need a *dessert season* of joy and communion with the Father, the Son and the Holy Spirit.

Part 3: Encounters that Made Me a Son

Becoming Love for Others

Leading the way in forgiveness and love is our greatest privilege as Christians. Christians should be the first to call out the true worth in others without concern of our own appearance. When people see true forgiveness displayed in front of them, the veil is very often lifted, and we can't even understand our former offenses. If I see you forgive before I do, or be strong when I would expect you to be weak, it moves me. I am impacted by your strength, even if your strength is really just His strength shining through you. In fact, somewhere in there, I know its proof of Him in you.

Love is truly our most abundant resource. Not only is it one of the most valuable, but it is also the most plentiful. More often than not, we get the seemingly expensive role of giving that love away without receiving it back immediately, if in our lifetime. We've heard that we give to receive, but sometimes, especially when the return feels low like this, we stop giving. The truth really is that the well is endless. Christians lead when they know that. Leaders look back on what Father God did for us, giving His son, giving us a new heart and communing with us through it. They look back on their salvation and by doing so they replenish their supply. We were reborn in abundant love and if we choose to recall it, we'll find we never left abundance and that well doesn't run dry.

We lead the world from our love, our unconditional love. We unbalance the deficits of poverty with love. We know we can always afford to boldly love, to love without recognition when we know that we are loved. When we have discovered heights, depths, and lengths of God's love for us. When others want to harm, but then see us doing the opposite, it is evidence that the dirge isn't the only song available.

If you're feeling the sunshine right now, you know that dirge phase you went through, or something like that, was a bit expensive. I've been in seasons where I thought the dirge was the only melody worth singing, but every time I can authentically sing a song of life, I know it's what I was born to do. My whole being comes to life. I was born to authentically sing the song of life in front of everyone. I am so supplied with love that brings life that I can actually sing until the whole world sings or at least to bring them the option.

I'm not talking about smiling all the time or something like that either. I'm talking about holding on to the things that bring you life, and letting go of what weighs you down. We know there is hope, so let it be; there is light, so let it shine; there is a God we can trust. There is a future! We can sing, "We ♪ are ♪ loved by the Father ♪" until the world hears and begins to sing along.

Part 3: Encounters that Made Me a Son

Prayer Activation

Take a moment with each of the following. Give yourself a minimum of 3-5 minutes to respond to each. Press in with a soft heart toward our loving Father. He will not hold back any good thing from you. Go for it.

When I say "Father" what do you see (a man with a beard, a light, a feeling of love, etc.)?

Write it down, be specific. If you don't understand ask God for clarity.

_____

_____

_____

Where do you see Him (in a room, on the beach, in a vision, in the past, etc.)?

Write it down, be specific and if you don't understand ask God for clarity:

_____

_____

_____

What is the Father doing there (is He speaking, is He smiling, is He holding you)?

Write it down, be specific and if you don't understand ask God for clarity:

_____

_____

_____

Part 3: Encounters that Made Me a Son

Ask Father God what He thinks about you. Write what He says down:

_____

_____

_____

If you feel rejected, unloved or any such things have manifested in your time here with Father God, ask Him what you are believing that is a lie. "Father God, am I believing any lies about myself or about you?"

_____

_____

_____

If you heard a lie, be sure to ask Father God what the truth is and write that down. Do this a few times if needed. Get it all out so you can be sure you're believing truth.

_____

_____

_____

If you didn't see, sense or feel anything during any of those previous questions, but did have an experience or encounter with any of the previous exercises, then ask Jesus or Holy Spirit if there is anyone you need to forgive. If you receive a name or see someone's face, then assume that is the person, even if it doesn't make sense. Forgive and release that person through the blood of Jesus to both break unholy bonds with them and wash clean anything you left with them, but now need back in order to live a life of wholeness. Take it back in prayer and receive it though the blood of Jesus. He sacrificed it all for you because He wanted you free and whole, so decide today to be free, to be loved.

Prayer Example (declare out loud if possible):

In Jesus name and with His strength and life I choose today to forgive _____ (say their name). I give back to them anything I took from them spiritually or emotionally. I give it backed washed in the blood of Jesus. Likewise, I take back anything I gave to them spiritually or emotionally also washed in the blood of Jesus.

If you've done this then go back now and try the exercise(s) again. Many will experience it completely differently. If you still don't experience the exercise differently, do not be discouraged. If it's helpful, ask again if there is anything blocking you from seeing, hearing, or sensing the Father in any way. If it's a wall, ask questions (what is the wall Lord? Why is it there? Is it safe to take it down? Ask if He wants to take it down with you. Ask for a tool and ask what

Part 3: Encounters that Made Me a Son

the tool represents). Many need to forgive their earthly dads before they can encounter the Heavenly Father. If that makes sense to you, then go through the prayer example again using your earthly father's name and personalize it for depth and sincerity.

If you still need help, I recommend contacting someone in your area's "Sozo Network" or a Christian Counselor. Find more information about sozo online at www.bethelsozo.com. Ask your local church leaders about Christian counseling or if they recommend any services online or locally. Otherwise, many resources are available online with accompanying reviews and statements of faith and doctrine available.

Did you have an encounter during this exercise? Or do you want to read about other encounters that people have had? Visit our Facebook group to tell others about it and spread the good news. See Appendix A of this book for help writing or filming your testimony. I believe that God wants to normalize the supernatural lifestyle of encounters daily and the thought of having a database of the supernatural activities of God thrills me to no end. I pray that you receive these encounter gifts abundantly. Please see Appendix A for more information.

Chapter 7
Encounters from His Kingdom

The church has always had a lot of encounters with truth and authenticity for me. The church, she is the Bride. Jesus gave everything for her rescue. When she is ready, there will be a wedding in heaven. The church isn't a building, a denomination or anything like that. It is a people chosen by God for the indwelling of His Holy Spirit. The church is every person who has been in a relationship with Jesus in history. The church is timeless and faceless. It's a movement; it's revival; it's the character of Jesus, the Kingdom of God and so much more.

My first experience with the Bride of Christ was a bit strange. It was about two weeks after my encounter in the park with the open vision, so I'm backing up again to move forward. New to the faith, I barely recalled how church worked from my youth experiences with it. I wasn't even there for church. I was there to see a friend speak.

Several weeks before, my life was at the peak of anxiety. I was working 80-hour weeks and following a dream I had to see the broken world fixed through business and economics. I was working for one of the world's greatest leadership organizations and had a ten-year plan for how I'd write a book and save the world. I was going to teach big companies how to be generous in order to increase sales. It was my dream job. I had it all. I was working in the custom consulting department, working with the most successful companies in the world. I thought I was in the bigtime, but God pulled me out of it.

After the open vision from chapter 4, I knew my life had changed, but I didn't understand how. There was this phone call though from a friend I had worked with at a community services nonprofit just a few weeks before the open vision. He asked me to help him build a new community service nonprofit with him and I told him I wasn't interested. It sounded fun, but I had my dream job, I thought. I did remember that we had both left that other job together and at the going away party, someone mentioned he was a "Man of the Cloth." I was shocked! I had been working with him for two years and didn't know he was a Christian or anything.

After the open vision, I went back to work. I felt a shift and I just couldn't work there. It was a struggle, because I thought that was my dream, but suddenly it didn't cut it for me. I became physically nauseous and just couldn't do my job. My supervisors noticed right away. It was a massive workload and suddenly I wasn't pulling it. It was like I couldn't.

Part 3: Encounters that Made Me a Son

About two weeks went by before they let me go. I knew it was going to happen and so all I could think about was my friend who had called. I wondered if he was a good speaker, because I knew if we were to start a nonprofit, he'd need to do most of the speaking for us. I remembered the "Man of the Cloth" comment, and so I called him and asked him if I could come visit his church to hear him speak.

I didn't know what God was up to at all. I wasn't even suspicious and so, of course, he said yes. My friend knew what was happening the whole time, but I thought of it like a business opportunity. I remember showing up to his Hispanic church with a briefcase kind of bag, a pen and pencil, ready to take notes like in a business meeting. Also, in a business meeting, you look for the best seat and so I noticed some empty seats up at the front. I went up to the pastor's wife, not knowing who she was and asked her to scoot over.

I was like a fish out of water. They started the worship music set and I was confused. I hadn't remembered this part at all from being a kid in church. But I had been a musician in a heavy metal band, so I was harsh on the band. I thought, *Why are they only using three chords?* and *Why didn't they spend more time practicing?!* I couldn't figure it out, but my friend finally went up to speak. The message began.

He spoke about "Relationship with Jesus" and I had never conceived of such a thing, but I had just had this open vision and so I wondered already if Jesus was who I had always heard him to be.

Somewhere near the beginning, I began crying and couldn't stop until the end. Even though we would eventually begin that nonprofit, this was the real reason I had come it seemed. After the message, I went up to him and dramatically grabbed his shoulders and said, "I need one of those!"

He said, "One of what's?" with a sly grin.

I said, "I need a relationship with Jesus!"

He laughed because he knew why I was there the whole time.

Part 3: Encounters that Made Me a Son

Learning that the Church is What Was Missing

The thing that was difficult for me over time was, why God didn't use me to help save the world? I had this great job and I was working with companies that could have changed the world economically to defeat poverty, but it seemed clear that He had called me out from that opportunity. Why? I wanted to know, and to make matters worse, the organization that my friend and I built together after I got saved eventually came to an unjust end. Why didn't God want me to change the world and help the poor? I asked the Lord and one day He told me. He said, "Josh, I don't want you to save the world. I want my church to save the world."

The church wasn't what I expected. It took me a long time until to even understand what worship was all about. I had to come close. It happened after a worship pastor found out that I was in that heavy metal band years before as a guitar player. He asked me over and over about coming to play in the band. I told him week after week that I couldn't and made up excuses to be polite.

But one day I told him the truth. I said, "Worship music is lame, and I don't even understand why you try. It's so boring..." I kept going and unloaded on him there.

When I finished, he paused and said, "So, do you want to come by on Wednesday for practice?" and handed me some chord charts.

I couldn't believe he still wanted me to come and play, but he knew what he was doing I guess. I took those charts home and as I learned the songs, I started to connect with them. I had something happening in me. I was feeling the presence of God. We practiced and I played on stage for the first time that next Sunday morning.

I immediately connected to God when I was up there. I realized that what I had been doing in band as a kid was always missing this third element. It was just us and the crowd in the metal band, but here it was both horizontal and vertical. It was the band, it was the congregation and it was heaven too. It was full. It was what had been missing from every kind of music I had ever known.

And just like that, the pendulum for worship music swung from one side to the other and I deleted and threw out every secular album I had in favor of only worship music from here on. I knew it was cliché, but all the other music seemed so worthless suddenly. I have always been a big music collector and so it was a lot of CD's and such, but I was sold. I had been missing a third connection to heaven and I wasn't going to let another song go by without that. Eventually

I found God in secular music too but it took time to come around. God doesn't live in our boxes, He does whatever He pleases.[25]

What the church did for me is it gave me a taste of heaven on earth. Church is filled with people and so it's not heaven, but it can be filled with it. Understanding more about church helps me connect with the idea that God truly wants His heaven on earth. He wants us to have what He has and now and here.

In church, people get saved, healed and delivered and they're taught Scriptures, they're given a sounding board for ideas, a safe place to practice the gifts of the Holy Spirit and so much more. Many have said rightly that it's not supposed to be a perfect place, but more like a hospital for the recovering needy souls out there. Every time I come to church, I am getting the opportunity to declare with everything that I am that I can't do it alone; I need you, church.

---

[25] *Psalms 115:3*

Becoming What Others Need

I tell this story about worship too, because I believe that the world is out there trying to figure out how to have fun and accomplish things, just like I was. They're out there building things like bands and doing things without God to the best of their ability.

It's not all they're doing. Sometimes people are out there doing straight evil things, but most of the time, they're more off the mark than in straight malice. Most drugs and alcohol are clearly counterfeits of the real thing. Religions outside of Christianity, movies, books, games, and so on – they all point to a need for the Savior. They're even doing good things without God. It's true. But like me, they probably don't know how much better it would be with God.

Christian television looks boring. Our services look liturgical and archaic, but if they knew how to build with God, they'd see the more. It was like a puzzle piece that went missing and I had tried to make the puzzle without it, but when I found that piece, I stopped lying about how it was already a full puzzle and began to celebrate the true completion of the puzzle.

The church can lead the way in making that vertical connection to God. That connection to God is endlessly portable. It can go anywhere and do anything. God isn't just influencing church, government, business, etc.; He's inviting those every mountain of influence into the fatted-calf party from the Luke 15 parable we read earlier. If we made our Christian lives about everyday life with God, then the availability of God would fill everything we do to overflow. We have to party with God everywhere we go.

It is our inheritance to have the full family of God, Holy Spirit and Jesus with us everywhere we go. For the added benefit of us all. They are what is missing from work and play, vacations and adventures. The church gives us that platform to heal and live with the Trinity in public with support. It's a place to learn to carry both the habitation and the visitation of God, like Graham Cooke talks about. God in us for me and God on us for them, like Bill Johnson talks about. Life for the world is horizontal, but not vertical. I believe we have that answer they seek for that missing puzzle piece in their lives. For us, it's not about judging the world. It's about loving the world. Billy Graham famously said, "It's God's job to judge, the Holy Spirit's job to convict, and my job to love."

Prayer Activation

Take a moment with each of the following exercise questions, prayers and activities. Give yourself a minimum of 3-5 minutes to respond to each.

When I say Church, what do you see, sense, or feel? Write it down.

_____

_____

_____

Did you have any trouble seeing or experiencing Church? If so, ask Jesus why (if you currently feel more connection to Father God or Holy Spirit you can ask any of them, just replace "Jesus" with their name instead). Say, "Jesus why can't I see your church?" and write that down, whatever He tells you. If it's a past church or some other church you've attended you see, ask Jesus if you need to

Part 3: Encounters that Made Me a Son

forgive that church. If it's a wall, ask Him if He wants to help you take it down. Keep asking questions until you hear from Jesus. Your relationship with church is a vital connection as a Christian. You need to be able to love the church without concern or judgement. The church isn't the building, it is the people. Many have used their positions to poorly steward the power it brings. It's time to forgive them anyway. Bless them and move on. Write down whatever Jesus tells you and work through it with him.

_____

_____

_____

If you feel hurt by the church, like you don't understand how or what Jesus will do with the church, ask Jesus what you are believing that is a lie. "Jesus, am I believing any lies about the church or about your love for your bride?"

_____

_____

_____

If you heard a lie, be sure to ask Jesus what the truth is and write that down. Do this a few times if needed. Get it all out so you can be sure you're believing truth.

_____

_____

_____

Did you have an encounter during this exercise? Or do you want to read about other encounters that people have had? Visit our Facebook group to tell others about it and spread the good news. See Appendix A of this book for help writing or filming your testimony. I pray that you receive these encounter gifts abundantly. Please see Appendix A for more information.

Part 3: Encounters that Made Me a Son

Part 3: Encounters that Made Me a Son

Chapter 8
Abundance, Encounters and Sonship

A Year of 365 Encounters

Hopefully by this point, you are believing the Lord for more encounters in your life and are already experiencing an increase in encounters. There's one more major encounter I received I'd like to tell you about. This encounter was made up of many encounters, lasted a full year, and when it was done, it left me with a fully cultivated, daily relationship with God, which at least to me, seems to be God's number one reason for all encounters.

In the introduction to this book, I mentioned the year God gave 365 encounters that followed along with a daily Bible reading plan my mom had given me years before. As much as I'd like to, I can't write a case-by-case account of those encounters I received that year because there was never enough ambition on my part to keep track of it all. The generosity of God is truly mesmerizing. While I cannot nail each day down for you, I will describe and give examples of the different types of encounters I experienced.

For example, I had *subjective* encounters (see chapter 1 for a description) where I was the only person who could ever appreciate them. A common manifestation of that was when I received a revelation that would cause me to change my direction that day. Others were *objective*, like when a person would get healed on the street after I felt led to pray for them.

I felt like I never knew when, how or where God would encounter me. I also didn't know how much or little time was needed or how much control I'd have, if any. In keeping me guessing, His real goal wasn't to catch me off guard, but I think it was to show me the manifold nature of His character Paul talked about in Ephesians.[26] The fact that they were always so unpredictable also made me feel safe from any notion that I was generating them somehow. That was an important peace for me to maintain, given that my analytical mind would have come in to shut me down had it felt the need.

It's not that He was insensitive to my daily life either. I was never truly embarrassed in front of others. He clearly cared for me throughout the process, but my options to shut them down was still

---

[26] *Ephesians 3:10*

further challenged, because I remembered praying that I wanted it all from Him. Apparently, he was looking for someone like that, and this is something I found that He looks for. He wanted someone who would receive Him, at any cost. At all cost.

Almost everything had to do with intimacy and knowing His Word. This manifold approach also showed me that He was the initiator, not me. This is an important detail as well. God is the giver; we should ask and expect, even lay our lives down for it, but God gets to do the giving here too. This is not a one-sided relationship, or if it was, it is no longer. He isn't looking for drones who have no personal response but just preprogramed yes's and no's. He's looking for us and who we are. It's a lot less about what He wants to change. It's about who He created us to be and How when we receive from Him, that gets healed and firmly established. He's challenging us to keep His Word in our hearts and not deviate from it so that we will be truly confident.

I surrendered to His discipleship, as clearly, He had an abundance of truth to show me. I allowed myself to be vulnerable to those encounters daily. I got excited about them. I felt like the angels at God's throne, exclaiming, "Holy, Holy, Holy," again and again. I was seeing so many aspects of God and His Word and they were all so very good! Every time I looked, I saw Him differently, and every time, it was astonishing!

There were also days when I felt too close to these encounters, like I would forget where I was and thought I might never come back. Sometimes they were moments, sometimes hours, sometimes they'd last through the night. But other times I missed it. I'd look back and see the days I missed reading and realize that each day lined up with an encounter. He was faithful even if I wasn't. It was unconditional again and again. Sometimes I'd even backtrack and receive multiple encounters all at once, remembrances of people and themes that took place on those days I had missed.

There was an occasional aspect of future forecasting, where I suspected what encounters I might have in the coming days. By the time that day's reading came, I was freshly prepared, but had forgotten most of my premonitions. I wasn't always right about stuff anyway, but the sense that I could trust Him to give me more encounters was the thing that was founded again and again.

Visions, touches, smells! I heard, I saw, I laughed a lot in fits—far outside of my personality. I was taken up, taken low; I was empowered, shaken. I was awakened and put to a rest. I was made to stand still or run ahead. There were so many things sorted out from my past. I was healed, delivered; so many ambitions and aspirations abandoned, and others adopted. I saw demons leave that had been in my family line for generations. Shame and guilt lost their grip on my soul forever. I still know they're options, but I don't have to receive them the way it felt like I once did. That deception was exposed! The stronghold broken for good.

It was shaping, forming and molding, but also empowering and strengthening to my core. I found strength as my soul and body began to find their connection to my spirit man. Everything was relevant, whether I was reading my Bible or working out. These things were not allowed to be compartmentalized. I was not a three-part being; I was just me. My spirit, soul and body were all the single object of His affections as one. They were not at odds with one another.

My flesh was clearly renewed when Jesus rose from the grave. I came up with Him, not as a warring individual myself versus myself, but as a new creation. My peace within was being established through His consistent presence. I came to a place where that was everything, again and again. Like Moses, I didn't want to go up from a place if He wasn't coming with me. He is what makes us whole and being whole is everything we need. From a place of wholeness, nothing is impossible, and we are with God.

Though my mind was frequently blown, I managed in my day-to-day, except for the occasional interruptions that did happen. I retreated to the bathroom, or to another room at times, stayed home from social events. I spent a lot of time in 2009 on my own, processing. A worthy investment to say the least. I was hidden. I was grateful, but also struggling to find a job or consistent work in the business I was building. That didn't feel like a blessing, but I wouldn't trade it, of course.

I'm an introvert mostly and so I deeply enjoyed that time in my private space, exploring, watching, expecting, and rehearsing the powerful moments I had with the Holy Spirit. I grew in my ability to receive encounters, and I still am growing now. The places He wants to go are so deep that there are often many layers to go through. In His great kindness though, He always went to great lengths to prepare my heart for the specific destinations He had in mind. Each and every encounter revealed how He existed in everything – how majestic He is, how eternal He is, all while teaching me how to be equipped in life.

The encounters were often revelations about who He is or who I was, or who Bible characters were. God clearly values identity! He wants soundness in our being, and we can find that when we look at identity the way He wants us to. Most of these encounters involved God and people, like the two commandments of love the Lord and love your neighbor. Even when it was wisdom or a manifestation that involved money or wisdom, it was generally about people. It was all so alarmingly natural and supernatural at the same time.

It was also never black-and-white ideas—quite the opposite. I would almost daily need to surrender my right to understand before I received the understanding, which at times happened months later. I didn't always arrive either. There are so many things that continue to leave me undone, and I'm left to ponder, or give them over to His wisdom. There were moments that seemed so strange or so different from everything I've ever understood. He was breaking my box and continues to do so today, though now my roots go much deeper as He has established me. If I get broken into pieces now, I am aware that He'll put me back together even stronger than before.

I suppose if I decided any of this made me a genuine authority, it would be a stumbling block. God wasn't establishing rules in me; He is always establishing things like trust, love and intimacy from me to Him. I'm open to God, and I believe He is constantly teaching me to be more open to Him everywhere. "Expanding the tent pegs" as they say. Territorially taking over every square inch of my heart while pouring out love and adoration on my entire world. God has enough love for the whole universe and if we'd let Him, He'd pour everything we can receive through us.

All of these encounters were, and continue to be, a form of *experiential discipleship coming straight from the Word*. I was learning to do what I understood my Father had done and is doing. I was learning to participate with what He is doing and saying. I found myself living the stories, themes, and messages of the Bible. Not such a big surprise really, but I never thought the Bible could be as relevant as it clearly is. It is simply what God is doing and saying on the earth today. There is a rhythm to it too, and it was like He was singing it over me so that I could hear Him all year long.

And today, I still seem to be traveling with that song. That's the thing. It's not just one year He's inviting us into. Rather, what I found was how willing He was to help me cultivate deeper connection to Him in my daily life. He is everywhere, and nothing is without purpose and meaning. But even when the purpose and meaning are outside of our grasp, He's still there offering us a feast of love and wisdom, purpose and destiny; Intimacy.

What's in Our Inheritance?

We are God's family. His heirs to everything. One day, all that we see and far more that we don't see will be ours. I feel certain heaven won't be boring at all. When He calls us good and faithful servants, He'll likely hand us the stars in His hand to steward. He'll be everywhere we go, with us in complete union. What He is giving us here is a taste of what we will become there.

However, there's this one little Scripture from the Lord's prayer that makes that far away reality closer than we can imagine. A lot closer than we're mostly comfortable with. When He told His disciples to pray for earth to be like heaven, He didn't hide heaven from us, He made a promise that we could see it. How else could we hope to see it on earth if we didn't even know what it looked like in heaven?

No, Jesus demonstrated what He was asking them to see. He healed the sick, lame and possessed like in heaven. He loved like in heaven. Can anyone be sick in heaven? It's not possible. How do we know? Because He showed us. He rested and enjoyed, made friends and gave hope. He went to wedding parties and church temples like heaven and so much more.

Our heavenly accounts aren't for heaven; they're for our lives now. Jesus wasn't storing up riches for His afterlife by doing a bunch of good deeds on earth. He was revealing a lifestyle of unity with the Father of heaven. We're not storing up riches for heaven where the streets are made of gold and there is no lack. We won't need it then! That isn't it.

We're being empowered to live out a life of the abundance of love on the earth, just like Jesus was. We're given the sounds of victory and expected to sing them out in how ever we do our lives. Just like in heaven, we have our Father here with us, completely available. Never leaving, never forsaking us. He is closer than a brother, closer than our skin. He is within the deepest places of us and we can expect that from Him. It's not entitlement, it's faith. The kind of faith that delivers a very real and completely purchased inheritance into our hands. Knowing Father God like Jesus knew Father God is the gift that brings heaven to earth. It's the conduit, the stairway. It's at hand.

Jesus' strength and power came from His access to heaven and Father God. Jesus saw unrighteous things and called out the lie that made them that way. He had seen the truth even from both His God and His human perspective. Jesus showed us how to live from our inheritance. He looked to heaven in front of the crowds, time and again. He pulled down what He saw there, and manifestations supplied the earth with the abundance He had access to. We too have that same access He had. He won that for us when He resurrected from the grave.

I've watched in my life when I have prayed for people and time and again, they will get a sense of my nearness to God. Hope will immediately appear, and that hope will open them up to heaven's resources. What we allow God to do in secret gives Him permission to do it openly. What God is doing in me is for the whole of creation.

I am experiencing an unlocked reality because of what Jesus did. It's the fatted calf party from Luke 15 and the Prodigal Son story and I'm taking it with me. God has prepared a table everywhere we go and learning to dine on His presence, and resources of hope, joy, love is our great supply for every situation. Even the older brother wanted to have a party. The Father went out running after him as well. The Father wanted everyone in the party together.

When I learn to feast at the table no matter where I am, I begin to live a lifestyle of both spirit and truth. It's the only worship worth following, the kind that's been somewhere and has come back carrying the breakthrough for everyone. A portable reality that I can carry anywhere and contribute. I have abundance when I've received abundantly. It's the only way. Guys, all of my personal supplies of hope, faith and love are finite. Limited. But I have access to infinite supplies when I go to the table that the Lord has set before me today.

I have to force irrelevance upon the Bible. Everything in there is relevant for us here. It is the source of His thoughts and the way He impacted our forefathers. The Bible is His love poured out in a cup and we are invited to drink its wine and eat its bread daily. The Bible offers us constant communion supplies. Will we eat and drink? That's up to us. Will we come into the fatted calf party and join in there? I haven't let a year go by without reading the Bible since. It's where I can be sure to meet with Him. He'll always have something to give me that He prepared beforehand for me.

We'll have to give up our powerless ideas and mindsets, things that have prevented us from receiving His fullness. We'll have to decide that what He says about Himself is actually true. We hear the music; we smell the barbeque. It's time to stop toiling around and go in and receive from our inheritance so that we can live from its abundance instead of for it.

It's more than we will ever need. It's an ever-expanding universe full of the things He already loves. Could it be that those things creating deficits in our lives are all disempowering lies we're believing? They are. There's nothing too broken that He can't restore, too lost that He can't find, too dark that He can't shine a light. His abundance is there to overwhelm all of that and more. He will share it all with us to the quantum depths of our being, all His love for us, and all His love with everything He created big and small. It's all ours to receive. It's far, far more than we'll need for ourselves.

Part 3: Encounters that Made Me a Son

Becoming a Son for Others

God is not short on encounters, my friends. God is overflowing with abundance and has more than enough for each and every one of us. Just look at the universe, how big and excessive it is. Quantum science has shown us something like a mirror of creation that goes in the other direction as well. Just as space is infinite, it seems the quantum reality is infinite too. Consider the abundance of it, any one of those planets out there holds enough metals and rock to build your home and everything in it over a million times.

God has a great amount of abundance right here on earth too. So much left for us to discover in our oceans, lands and skies. There is no end to His resource and supply, both above and below. It's available on every side of us. These things are meant to declare this to us. We are supposed to look at God's natural creation and discover truths about His nature and the way He thinks. One thing is overwhelmingly clear, if we are paying attention. He is abundant!

With such an abundant God, can it be that we have avoided receiving? That He isn't the stingy one, but rather far more generous than we can imagine? It has to be. Where's my heart at in this? Having had one bad experience defined by lack, do I allow that to color all my other experiences? God overwhelms His lovers with His abundance when we expect it to be there. It's a shift in our thinking, though. He is on the edge of His seat to teach us to be receivers of His abundant encounters. These lessons come straight from Him. It's very exciting, a favorite topic of His I believe.

I had a dream on the first day of my year of encounters. It was the morning of January 1, 2009. I was an older version of me in a place somewhere in Denver, Colorado where I'm yet to visit, outside of this dream. Everyone there was operating in their unique gifts. Everyone was completely alive in Christ. We shared everything together too, and had all things in common. We hadn't earned this by working toward each other.

We had been given this because we were all so fully alive and devoted to knowing Christ personally. We were so connected to Jesus individually, that we were fully alive and connected to each other through His oneness. Our individuality remained intact, but wasn't a dividing factor because His oneness made us all one.

The dream showed how He was endlessly establishing His manifold reality for us to see ourselves as the unique individuals He's created us to be. That ultimately, there is only one Christ and His oneness is the very thing that will make us all one. He was showing me how His desire to make us one will manifest into reality,

Part 3: Encounters that Made Me a Son

and He declared it over my lifetime through this dream. Unity without uniformity kind of thing. In the dream we were all unique but completely united by Jesus.

It was deeply challenging to my soul to accept that this was possible *within my own lifetime*. I wanted to, but I didn't know how. Like Sarah laughed about having a child at such an old age, [27] I laughed at the idea that the church could be anything other than divided. That church life could be this abundant reality. I had to trade in the limited way I thought to make the leap over to believing for abundance. This extremely abundant reality seems far off to this day, but every time I think of it, I am challenged to believe it more. I am being stretched and there is a difference in my capacity to receive the unity God will pour out today compared to when He gave it to me originally. Maybe like Sarah, I will one day help birth such a revival experience in unity but at the time I could hardly believe for it. Honestly, it was a little frightening.

The dream was so real I woke up in a sweat. I heard the Lord talk to me internally and say, "Don't be afraid Josh..." but I was afraid.

---

[27] *Genesis 18:12*

He said, "...In fact, any time you feel fear knocking, I want you to clap your hands three times. When you do this, I'll have *all* of heaven clap with you." He emphasized "all."

I gave it a shoot right then, I clapped three times and from the first clap my eyes were opened to the presence of heaven all around me. I witnessed all of heaven clapping in unison with me. It was thunderous and no fear could withstand it. Why did He think so much of me?! I still don't know, but I learned through the course of the year that it was wrong for me to reject it. He's giving us all He has. If we lack capacity to receive, He will help us with that as well.

False humility, whatever it is that shuts down His ability to give to me, has to go. It might sound weird, but I'm still finding ways to avoid His gifts. I'm still finding ways to make the turn to receive them as well.

The encounters didn't end after the 365 days. I still have frequent encounters, but those encounters followed that daily Bible reading plan I had, day after day, until the end. In addition to feeling a deep connection to many details of the Bible, I was cultivating daily relationship with the Lord. His presence doesn't leave me.

I know why Moses wouldn't leave without Him, and it isn't some kind of selfishness. It is because we were created to be loved, and once we've experienced His presence, we have to have more of it to fill the space it created when it came. We are sons and daughters. As we experience Him we are stretched and shaped and molded to be more like Him. He is abundant. Nothing else can be as abundant as He is and so we are left with a heart that only He can

Part 3: Encounters that Made Me a Son

fill. With a torn veil and complete access, each moment we experience Him stretches us more and we experience the reality of the glory to glory lifestyle. This is our inheritance, our sonship. It's a one-way ticket into a unified family. When others see us walking in contrast to the lack, they want it deep. It's unlike anything else out there. It's what we were all made for. We were made for abundance.

Prayer Activation

Take a moment with each of the following exercise questions, prayers and activities. Give yourself a minimum of 3-5 minutes to respond to each.

When I call *you* a son or daughter, what do you see, sense, or feel? Write it down.

_____

_____

_____

Did you have any trouble seeing or experiencing yourself as a member of God's family? If so, ask Father God why. Say, "Father God why can't I see myself in your family?" and write that down, whatever He tells you. If you see a past you, you didn't like, you might need to forgive yourself. If it's Father God you see, ask Father

Part 3: Encounters that Made Me a Son

God if you need to forgive Him. If it's a wall, ask Him if He wants to help you take it down. Keep asking questions until you hear from God. For some it's difficult to admit the need to forgive our Heavenly Father. He, of course, doesn't need our forgiveness. He knows He's sinless. We need it though. We need to release ourselves from the unforgiveness we've held against Him. If you see you as the problem, then ask Jesus why He'd give His life for you. Ask Him how valuable He thinks you are. Give time for Him to answer.

_____

_____

If you feel like there isn't enough and like poverty and lack are keeping you from your inheritance; if you feel like your distracted by your job, unable to rest or too busy, ask Father God, "Father God, am I believing any lies about abundance or about Your supply for me as an individual?" Write down what He tells or shows you.

_____

_____

If you heard a lie, be sure to ask Father God what the truth is and write that down. Do this a few times if needed. Ask about lies and if you get one, ask about truth and exchange the lie. Get it all out so you can be sure you're believing truth about abundance.

_____

_____

_____

Did you have an encounter during this exercise? Or do you want to read about other encounters that people have had? Visit our Facebook group to tell others about it and spread the good news. See Appendix A of this book for help writing or filming your testimony. I pray that you receive these encounter gifts abundantly. Please see Appendix A for more information.

Part 3: Encounters that Made Me a Son

PART 4
There is Enough

Part 4: There is Enough

Chapter 9
Repentance is a Lifestyle

We Repent

As Christians, we hear a lot about repentance, but we hear of it mostly as a moment of surrender. A single passing moment. But what if it's a lifestyle? What if it's a way of thinking and being every day? Better yet, what if it's also something that will fill you with joy daily!

Humiliation, self-abuse, penance, and self-hatred are all very inaccurate synonyms for repentance. We have to get it straight that repentance and punishment are not synonyms either.

I believe the idea of "repentance" is about our mind receiving and making a covenant with the beating heart and rhythms of heaven. It's about our willingness to give up our right to understand everything, our right to be perfect, our right to even carry on without feeling inspired to do so by our relationship with

God. It's about our willingness to come to God with nothing and admit that even though we're worthless without Him, He sees worth in us and we see and agree that His worth for us makes us truly valuable.

It's about waiting for the Lord to teach us what living is really about, where it comes from, how to do it, how to love it, and how to be. The happiness that comes from joy flows from the constant revelation of the total and finished work of Christ. It is the victory that is complete, and with it has come a new identity for each of us because He shares every part of it with us personally, until it defines us. Repentance is about receiving this. If we can't receive from the Lord then we can't repent. There is no repentance without receiving His alternative.

Condemnation is the opposite. It's when there are no options for change. Condemnation is the language of lies that every devil speaks. But repentance is conviction and offers us a redeemed option to live and move forward, away from the corruption of our current state. If there are no options, then it's not conviction and if it's not conviction then we cannot repent. All we can do is hate ourselves, which many do wholeheartedly.

> *"Saying we love God and secretively loathing ourselves is the ultimate contradiction. Loving your true self is loving God."* Randall Worley *(Tweet from 2018)*

Part 4: There is Enough

Don't let this sneaky vanity of loathing yourself win your moments. True repentance has to do with loving ourselves enough to be humble toward God and all His ways. He even keeps it mysterious *for* us rather than *from* us so that we can stay away from such pride and self-loathing. This might seem upside-down, but what I want to share is that we cannot repent if there are no options to change. Those options have everything to do with our good God. That's why there's so much joy in repentance. He's only ever asking us to be more like His Son Jesus. Even if we think that's impossible He never will, or else He wouldn't have sent Jesus to us. What isn't possible for us to do alone is completely possible to do with God in relationship.

Show Me Your Face God

I'll never forget my experience of reading the Scripture where it says, "Be ye perfect as my Father in heaven is perfect." That's Matthew 5:48 KJV. I dramatically dropped my Bible to the floor and told the Lord out loud, "I can't. I can't be a Christian and no one else can either. No one is innocent like You are."

I meant it. I thought I'd never read the Bible again. Obviously, the standards were completely unreachable. I had only recently been saved. Thanks to the supernatural, I now knew God was real, but with this Scripture, I felt convinced I couldn't cut it, and neither could anyone else. There were no options and His standards were clearly unreachable.

I wasn't wrong. A week must have gone by when I found myself in a service, thinking I'd come to say my goodbyes. In that service, I heard the Holy Spirit through the man preaching. When he said the name Jesus, the Holy Spirit whispered a healing truth to me, He said, "Jesus was perfect."

Part 4: There is Enough

My apartment was a short walk from that little church, and I left the service to go re-read the Scripture where I'd left off. I couldn't believe it. It was right there in Jesus' audience. Jesus was speaking to *religious* leaders, people who were so unbendable, so rigid, so pious, they had conceived that following the laws brought them perfection. They believed they were perfect in what they were doing to follow rules, but Jesus, knowing that what doesn't bend breaks, takes it up a notch and says, "...as my Father in heaven is perfect." Much like the scene where Jesus tells them to cast the first stone if they haven't sinned, they knew this was another level of perfection, unattainable from our human effort.

I saw it, even if they didn't. They, and we, are lost without Jesus because Jesus was perfect *for* us. Jesus wasn't keeping perfection *from* us, up and above us, out of our reach, but had already become the sacrifice we couldn't achieve, *for* us. He handed us His own perfection by becoming *our* sacrifice. We are perfect, even like His Father is perfect, because *Jesus is perfect*.

We don't have the ability to generate this level of perfection. Even if we never sinned, if we didn't know Jesus' perfection, ours would be "like filthy rags".[28] The NIV says in 2 Corinthians 5:21 that "God made him who had no sin to be sin for us, so that in him we might *become the righteousness of God.*" There would have been no

---

[28] *Isaiah 64:6*

end to the system of sacrifice God gave Moses for the temple if it weren't for Jesus being the perfect sacrifice. The Mirror Bible says in that same Scripture, *"He took our sins and we became His innocence."*

Could it be that we didn't even understand what God meant by perfect? We pretty much equated it with being a matter of right vs. wrong, or good vs. evil. We figured it had to do with the tree of the knowledge of good and evil, of our own ability to discern judgment, but Jesus was the Perfect that God was referring to all along. If we have Jesus, then we have perfect. If we are without Jesus, then we are simply without perfect. This is not a finite understanding of judgment. Jesus is the judgment here and the Tree of Life that brings eternal life.

This is why we needed a new covenant that brought us face to face with the eternal Father. Jesus paid the price so we could enter into the Holy of Holies, a place filled with the perfect face of the Father, so that what we could behold, we would become. This is repentance – to become what we behold, and that journey is our Lord's definition of perfect. He's like a mom watching her baby take his first steps and fall down and get back up again. She takes in a deep inhale to slowly release it. Under her breath she says, "He's perfect."

I love this from the Mirror Bible of 2 Corinthians 3:18:

> "The days of window-shopping are over! In [Jesus] every face is unveiled. In gazing with wonder at the blueprint of God displayed in human form, we suddenly realize that we are looking into a mirror, where every feature of his image articulated in Christ is reflected within us! The Spirit of the Lord engineers this radical transformation; we are led from an inferior mind-set to the revealed endorsement of our authentic identity."

That is a lifestyle worth living! This repentant transformation occurs as we look with intention at the object of our worship. We look directly at His face daily so that we will die and be raised back again in His image! We become Him as we worship Him, thanks to what Jesus has done. Not through acts or works; it's through relational connection with Christ so that He births His innocence within us. Repentance is giving up entirely on the notion of us controlling anything past our own ability to choose Jesus. We worship Christ, we know Christ, we become christ (little "c"). This is the lifestyle of repentance.

God seems to define perfection as *anything reconciled to Him*. To be reconciled, it seems, is to have been handed perfection as a gift. It is finished before we even start being restored. Restoration comes later. We might think perfection is when we're completely like Jesus, but the perfection actually occurs when we surrender in the first place. We're perfect while we are being transformed into His likeness.

Uniformity is not perfect. Beauty isn't perfect and there's a lot of false definitions out there we seem to give to this idea of perfection that are just not in God's definition. One thing is for sure, however, and that is that being perfect has nothing to do with our effort. It's throughout the Scriptures, in stories and themes from Cain and Abel, to the entire book of Hebrews that calls us into rest. Nowhere are we released to make ourselves perfect, because we can't. We are completely dependent on Jesus for our source of righteousness. That's okay though, because we win big, not just because it feels like we skipped a step, but because we get Jesus. He is our perfect sacrifice.

Part 4: There is Enough

My Life Is Yours Jesus

In Exodus, Nadab and Abihu, the sons of Aaron, offered a "strange offering" and immediately died. In the Amplified Bible's commentary, Frances Siewert gives us the description of this type of offering. She said it's as if our dad was a professional painter, but Nadab and Abihu came along and added some strokes to one of his pieces without permission. What they did was nearly identical to other offerings, but they didn't wait for God's instructions. No, they took all the initiative without any instruction. They assumed they didn't need the relationship He was offering through the sacrifices. They thought they knew how to do it and could just give offerings without God's direction. I've heard the phrase lately from various teachers including Justin Stockman who say, "They wanted the Kingdom without the King."

Frances reminds us that a lot of us can relate to what they did in principle. Those sons died right there; their trespass was irreconcilable any other way. The seat of Painter had already been taken; there simply wasn't room for them on the eternal throne of God to be God. I think it's Frances Chan who said to someone who came to him to complain about their worship experience. He said, "It's okay. We weren't worshiping you," to the person. Harsh, but point made.

When we take up our Christian lives without faith and worship, we have to call the shots. It won't be long before we have to die again, because we'll find there isn't life in that kind of perfect. It's a finite well that we're comparing to a well that never runs dry.

Mimicking Jesus won't work either. We're all invited to take up our cross like Jesus, but to try to do that exactly like Jesus, as opposed to following the principles He laid out won't get us closer to God. Can you imagine if someone hung themselves on a cross on top of Mount Golgotha, inside the church that now stands there (Church of the Holy Sepulchre)? It's ridiculous, even if it would make them perfect to do so, it would exclude all the rest of us; there's no relationship or invitation for anyone. A kingdom without a king isn't an option.

The cross already happened. The truth is we get to be who God created us to be through the inspired life that now lives on the inside of us. Just gaze upon it, and joy everlasting begins overflowing from the abundant supply of His face.

Obviously, we don't all end up looking and acting the same. The life of Christ isn't about uniformity, but about unity. Like a prism displays an endless array of color, we reflect the Lord as we come face to face with Him. Where the Spirit of the Lord is, there is freedom.

The life of Christ in you is the opportunity to be who you were created to be. It's not a still frame of who Jesus was, but a moving life of who He was resurrected to be through you/us. This is a much more fluid understanding than what we seemed to believe has ever been acceptable. This is the lifestyle we are invited into, though. A life of nonassumptive and continuous transformation. A lifestyle of repentance.

Repentance is more like a heartbeat, a wavelength, a rhythm of living. It's sonship. It's being moldable because He's our Daddy in heaven. Becoming a Christian should not be the end of our repentance, but the beginning of it. Our Christian life is a journey we engage in, not a place we arrive to.

Repentance is a lifestyle of joy and wonder. We worship, we know Him, we become Him. In that order. Repentance is a vulnerable way of living our life. We live wide open to God. Openness isn't dangerous; it's the only path to growth. It's painful at times, but openness to God is the only way. It's even the way, the truth and the life. We have to be opened to seeing the face of God in everything there is because He made everything and it all will be reconciled to Him, even though it kills us.

I've mentioned this before, but God's face does kill us. The face of God has never stopped killing us, and thankfully. God promised it would on Mount Sinai to Moses, after he asked God to show him His glory. But it is through Christ's resurrection that we are now entering into an eternal reality of Christ-life.

I know I died when I saw the standard. I was no longer a Christian, and fully realized that no one could ever be "perfect," as my culture had defined it. I died in the face of that truth. But He came with the gift He'd given. "Jesus is perfect," He said, and the breath entered back into me as I looked on the face of the Living God and I worshiped. My death purified me and made me like Christ through the repentance it set in motion. I was able to live and look at a real God because there is a real Perfect and it was never me sacrificing my right. It was always Christ giving me a right to change and to transform into who He was and is and is to come.

Repentance is a unique relationship with the Father that we are invited into. It's the place where we get to become what we are reading in the words of the Bible. We become the Bible because Christ became it. This is a lifestyle of repentance, not because it takes a lifetime, but because that is the invitation. The invitation is to live a life unplanned by us, but ordered step by step by the Lord Almighty.

We are invited into a living word, not a lifeless corpse, but a live Jesus, seated in heavenly places. We are even there with Him now, but we must have options if we are to experience anything other than what we know. We must learn the song of repentance as it flows out from heaven and sing along here on earth.

Until we do there won't be enough. Cause we won't walk in His purpose for us. We'll miss the mark and why! We know that we

Part 4: There is Enough

don't know, but if we will admit we don't and trust Him, we will be free to be who He made us to be. He's worthy of it all, my friends!

Prayer Activation

Take a moment with each of the following exercise questions, prayers and activities. Give yourself a minimum of 3-5 minutes to respond to each.

When you say, "I repent," what do you see, sense, or feel? Write it down.

_____

_____

_____

If you say, "I repent. I want to only do what you, Lord God do and say what you say, and I am open to do that today and every day. You are my Lord Jesus." What do you see, sense or feel? Did it feel possible? Did it feel a long way off?

_____

_____

_____

If it did feel a long way off or impossible, this is pretty normal, but ask the Lord to empower you today. Say, "Lord God, am I believing a lie about my ability to Hear you and see You?" If He says "yes"... ask Him the lie and then ask Him the truth to replace that lie and write the truth down here:

_____

_____

_____

Did you have any trouble feeling joyful repentance? If so, ask Lord God. Say, "Lord Jesus, why can't I feel joy in your gift of repentance?" and write that down, whatever He tells you. Work it out with Him. Keep asking questions that He prompts you to ask. Make sure you have the space and time for this exercise, If this isn't the time or place, write down a time and place when you will come back and complete it later. This could help you commit.

_____

_____

_____

Ask, "Lord Jesus, are there any lies I'm believing about you as my Lord?"

_____

_____

_____

If you heard a lie, be sure to ask Jesus what the truth is and write that down. Do this a few times if needed. Get it all out so you can be sure you're believing truth.

_____

_____

_____

Did you have an encounter during this exercise? Or do you want to read about other encounters that people have had? Visit our Facebook group to tell others about it and spread the good news. See Appendix A of this book for help writing or filming your testimony.

Part 4: There is Enough

I pray that you receive these encounter gifts abundantly. Please see Appendix A for more information.

Part 4: There is Enough

Chapter 10
There is Enough

Developing an Abundance Mindset About Encounters

I had an open vision just the other day, first thing in the morning. The Lord opened up a whiteboard right in front of me, but it was slanted. With a Sharpie, He wrote on it, "Good, Better and Best" from the bottom of the board up with "Best" at the top of the board. He smiled at me and said, "Everything here is good, but what you need is what is best. I want you to have your very best life, not your good life and not your better life, but your best life."

He was trying to help me with my boundaries in life, as at this time, I am stretched a bit thin. I've got two full time jobs. I'm working on this book. I play worship music from time to time for my church and I have a social life. It's abundant! Or is it? The reality is that I just have a problem saying, "no" to things I want to do, but don't have time for. You see God has plenty that is good for us, but what He wants for us is for us to want His very best. He's worthy of that too.

If I think about it, all through my life I have internally tasted the fruit of whatever wisdom I followed. Early in my life, I gave myself to hopelessness and followed in what I perceived to be its wisdom. This perception gave way to conception again and again, in ways that built upon each other. I went from bad to worse.

The same is true from my salvation. As I gave myself over to hear and conceive, I watched as fruit would appear, lifting me higher rather than lower. Hopelessness gave birth to sin and debauchery, and hope gave birth to life and new glories that expanded my capacity.

I witnessed God's ability and strength to heal, save and deliver me. These paths that I witnessed from dark to darker and from light to lighter are like road maps of hope that I can believe for the world around me. The world needs to be saved, healed and delivered. Our society has been given over to hopelessness, but I have seen how hope can change that direction.

What God did in me, He has enough abundance that He can do it for the world. He can even give the world His very best. If I perceive this on any level, then from that level, I can conceive of the hope that the world needs. Are you getting how powerful this is? God is equipping us through our witness. And He's still giving us choices to make. Choices that can honor His abundant generosity.

Part 4: There is Enough

Father God never expected you to be the generator of trust and love. He first loved us and gave us access to His supply. We have access when we perceive it. Have you witnessed God come through for you? When you have, you now know something about His ability to come through. If He comes through for you, will He not come through for others too? It's an obvious "yes" that's been a bit repetitive through this book, but it's really one of the very best revelations I have to offer you here. I pray you grab it.

To hammer just a little more, consider this – our human ability to love and trust is very short and finite compared to God's ability to. By perceiving God's ability within us, we conceive God's ability for the world around us. With this partnering relationship and the access it brings, you now have the ability to build your faith that He always comes; that He's always there.

You won't be one of the folks hearing lightning when others are hearing the voice of God[29]. You'll hear and see and even help others to do the same. Your capacity to receive every kind of encounter will grow, and your conception of what God has done in you will release the very best that heaven has to offer earth.

---

[29] *Acts 9:7 when the men with Paul didn't hear the voice that Paul heard.*

Spiritual Muscle Memory

The truth about encounters is that they are forgettable.

What? Why?!

I don't know. All I know is that both subjective and objective encounters are frequently forgotten, not just by me, but even entire communities of witnesses. If encounters aren't valued, written down, and rehearsed, they seem to rather easily disappear. Just think of all the times the Israelites would go back to worshiping golden calves. A lot had taken place to get them to forget the promises of God they had believed. God may have rescued them from this same sinful mindset just a few generations back but here it was again. To the reader, it's only a couple of pages, rather than decades or centuries and so we tend to be a bit harsh toward them. But still, how could they forget?

It's like someone who has a habit of walking with a limp. This limp is due to some kind of injury that put their body out of alignment. If they go to the chiropractor and get adjusted and for the first time, they're able to walk, there is a good chance they may fall back out of alignment. Sometimes sooner rather than later. This is why doctors ask us to keep coming back. If the patients don't keep going for adjustments, there's a good chance the muscles that once supported the injury become dominant. At the same time, those muscles that did not support the area before the adjustment can easily fall back into their secondary position. The person then resumes walking as if they have the injury when, in fact, they no longer do.

Why do we forget? I believe it has something to do with our ability to continually experience this alignment with the Father. If we begin to fall back on our everyday patterns, then it's almost like the experience never took place. Our continued experience post-encounter is not like the encounter itself, and so we end up with no use or place for it. It's very much like the old cliché, if we don't use it, we lose it.

My close friend, Felipe, and I once witnessed with our eyes what could only be the hand of the Lord under the tight t-shirt of a young man who went up for prayer for multiple slipped discs in his spine. What we saw was as unbelievable as it was undeniable. It was clearly a hand with distinguishable knuckles maneuvering something right where this man's lower spine was. He was completely healed of back pain in that moment.

Felipe and I had witnessed it from opposite sides of the aisle where we were serving as ushers. I walked over to Felipe and asked,

"Did you just see what I saw?!" He looked back at me and nodded with a somewhat frantic, "I sure did" look on his face.

We both witnessed a very real glory encounter this man had, and we witnessed it objectively. The man too was a witness, not of the hand, but of the healing. The man told us he simply felt peace and tingles in his spine, but the pain had vanished. I saw the man years later and he still had his healing.

At the event, Felipe and I went back and forth briefly about the possibility of deception, but we could not find a reasonable way to dismiss the hand moving around under that tight t-shirt. This man wasn't an aspiring magician and even if he was, this trick wouldn't have been possible without putting a hole in his torso. We landed without a place to put such a shocking experience. The Bible might call it a wineskin. This wine had no place to go. Neither of us had ever thought something so clear could be seen by one witness, much less the both of us!

Shockingly however, just two years later, while in a conversation with a mutual friend about it, Felipe didn't remember it! I had to remind him. I asked, "How is it possible that you forgot this?!" Once he recalled it, he told me he didn't know, but now that I had reminded him, he recalled it perfectly.

Repetition builds our ability to do something with ease. This is true with our muscles. I believe spiritual muscle memory is a good concept to help us understand how it is possible that we forget amazing encounters like this one. Without a wineskin, these encounters are poured out, but ultimately not ingested.

Without a faith to contain our encounters, we don't keep them around very long. As my value and awareness grew for encounters, the frequency grew. And awareness builds faith for every kind of encounter. I even start looking at other people's encounters and realize I can have those too. The really wild thought is that if this can happen for my consciousness, it can happen for an entire community's consciousness. Having awareness is the container that can take us into subjective and objective encounters. Getting that awareness is the very process I'm inviting you to join me in, here in this book.

I've had far more encounters than I can remember, even before I started reading through the Bible and had the 365 encounters. But as I read through that year, I found that the Lord partnered with me and helped me establish the necessary "memory stones" so to speak, using the Word itself.

If I went back to read a Scripture, I'd recall how He connected me to that Scripture. However, there were still casualties when I didn't return to them frequently enough. Some stuck, some did not. Perhaps four to five hours each day would have sufficed to recall all of the encounters through Scripture, but that's difficult to do with the busyness of life and I lost many.

Keeping up with what I can is like mental gymnastics, in a good way. Obstacles always show up to help us forget, and we have to either maneuver them or become distracted by life. Even an unforgettable, life-changing encounter can be lost in the ocean of everyday experiences. We go back to religion, or form, rather than allowing the memory stones to build expectation. Memory stones that build faith in a God who is generous with His love and nearness, His connection to us.

I believe that as we unwrap this gift of abundant encounters, God will help us build spiritual muscle memory so we can continually testify of the presence of available encounters – testifying to both others and ourselves. If you expect encounters every day, you position yourself to receive from whatever the Lord has prepared for that day. The Word helps us with cues, and before we know it, we're a spiritual athlete, moving around in our day.

We have endless opportunities to come into close, tangible contact with the Lord. Jesus didn't jump into ministry until he was thirty years old. When Jesus was a kid, he grew in favor with God and man. It was a process. Confidence is something that can be established freely, and I want us to have faith for that. We can feel secure in our ability to encounter God. I believe that while you, too, may forget more encounters than you remember, you will also increase your ability to receive encounters in every moment. It's not something easily achieved at first, but it's not a competition. You can rest assured that over time, we become very astute to the opportunities He lays out for us. Our appetite grows voracious!

To this day, I have near constant encounters. It's not that the frequency has increased, and it's not because I've pleased God and now He rewards me. It's because I respond. When I first had these encounters, it was intense. I often had to position myself for an encounter as if someone were throwing fifty pounds at me and I

Part 4: There is Enough

had to somehow hold it up. In time, and with repetition, fifty pounds doesn't feel that heavy to someone who lifts it. Today, the frequency of encounters hasn't diminished, but my ability to receive them has expanded. I have grown in my capacity.

An Ecosystem from Gratitude

I often have encounters when I hear a testimony of someone else's encounter. It's often the same or very similar to their encounter. It's as if God sees the desire of my heart and rushes in to deliver it. He can't even resist our gratitude.

> "Yes, all things work for your enrichment so that more of God's marvelous grace will spread to more and more people, resulting in an even greater increase of praise to God, bringing Him even more glory! 2Cor.4:15TPT

Thank You Lord!

Selah~

I heard one testimony from two different people where they were pressing in to receive that face-to-face experience with God through worship. As they looked at His face, it was like their face merged with God's. Soon I found myself in worship at Bethel Atlanta and I saw His face! I remembered the prophecy and as our faces came toward each other, my nose dipped into God's face like a pool of water. I saw His face in the water's reflection. As I moved forward, God's nose began wrapping around mine and became my nose – His cheeks, then mouth, eyes, hair, ears, until I was completely wrapped in His face. When I opened my eyes, I was looking through His eyes and speaking with His mouth. What I was hearing was purity and what I was seeing was love and passion for the world.

Abundance is the ability to receive the blessings He brings and to have the capacity to let them lift us even higher than before. This is like an eco-system or an economy of encounter wealth. Without the stewardship of testimonies, we don't grow. If we build our ability to steward what He gives, then we will have more when He brings more. For example, if we are grateful for a time, but quickly forget our testimonies, we don't write them down or tell them, our poor stewardship of what we have been given keeps us in a defeating cycle. Rather than grow, we are just living for the next miracle.

Even though He blesses us frequently, our capacity never increases and so we never really see abundance. We're falling in the same trap the Israelites did in the desert. The only way to tip the scales towards abundance here is if we begin to steward and build our capacity to steward the testimony towards sustainability first and then abundance and overflow. We have more than enough for ourselves. We have more than enough for our church or even our denomination of churches. There is enough, but we have to be able to apply the testimony.

If we are all having encounters and God is giving encounters abundantly to everyone, then there is enough to overwhelm all the "not enough" out there. Lack is a thing of the past, and everyone can see the abundance on the sons and daughters of God. How can we do this? It's simple. Write them down and share your testimonies so others can be grateful and believe in the God that delivered you, saved and healed you.

They can connect with the God who inspires innovation and has all the answers they need to walk in their purpose. So many are running on fumes, or at a deficit in God. Be generous! Sharing your experiences will bring about a kind of eco-system from their gratitude. A healthy eco-system like this would help people know God is real for themselves. They would have more and more subjective and objective experiences and people would learn new ways to encounter God and to know Him more.

The only reason that most things are valuable is because we've assigned the value. The thing about encounters is that the world needs to understand the value of Emanuel. He is God with us, not God away from us up in the sky and many don't know that. Can you imagine with me what the world would be like if everyone had a relationship with the God who loves and created them? He wants it and believes He can achieve it. We've seen Him do it in us, we believe He can do it in others. That's enough. There is more than enough.

Part 4: There is Enough

Together We Can Overwhelm all the World's Deficits

Our revelation that "there is enough" can grow louder than this worldly distorted truth that "there's not enough" we've been hearing everywhere these days. When we begin to live as prosperous souls in front of the world, united and blessed, we'll spark what some have called an "evangelism of jealousy."

It's not that we're not out there doing missions and sharing the Gospel with the lost. It's that we're doing everything, especially that, with the Lord. We have to know that we know, from small to large, we have to celebrate our oneness. Whether it's picking up a piece of trash or praying and receiving healing for our cancer. We need to continually congratulate ourselves saying, "Yeah, that's what revival looks like!" Or "I look like Jesus!" or whatever resonates and brings real joy forth.

While visiting India this past December, the Holy Spirit began to talk to me about America. He said, "America needs to stop being shameful about how great it is as a nation with money. Never in the world has there been a greater steward of finances than that nation." He showed me how where we should have allowed humility to declare this truth, we've chosen shame again and again. Shame that we have so much, shame that we are great. We've chosen shame over humility.

Humility can generate generosity that will build a better world. Shame tells us to simply stop doing what we do so well. America needs to just be who it is, a great nation that is an excellent steward of money. That is what would serve the world best.

Other nations have their great gifts, and those gifts are put there to supply for well-being everywhere. Nations like India clearly have a great gifting for administration and government. I have no doubt that many are shaking their heads, but I'm not saying the gift is fully manifested, I'm saying it's there. It's hard for a thing to be beautiful if no one ever calls it beautiful. That it is there is unquestionable.

The gift of administration has flourished in India for millenniums. With so many people, so many needs, India relies on administration constantly. America doesn't handle crowds like India does. It's not our gift. America doesn't have crowds like India does. People in India come to every party there is. Everyone together, and there are a lot of everyone's! That people-administrative muscle has been stretched torn and rebuilt to a massive extent America couldn't dream of. They could teach the USA about community and festive gatherings. They really have so much! If they knew it and walked in humility toward these strengths, it could be one of the most valuable resources on the planet.

Many nations seem to have strengths in everything from math to playfulness to media and so on. Can we imagine a world where we build together using our strengths as nations? That's all I'm trying to cast a vision for here. A world where the strengths of the nations were brought to a common communion table with our loving Jesus. Every weakness would be swallowed up by the strengths of our Lord. Even if we can't, God can. This is a world where there is enough – an "all things in common" world like the dream. Our unity wasn't found in our sameness, but in our diversity looking at Jesus' oneness.

I literally had an attack of weighty revelation when the Lord asked me if I thought the church could be united as one. I knew there was something behind the question if He was asking it. Then I realized it was Him Who was asking it. I said, "There's no way we could do that Lord, but You Lord, You could unite Your church. I believe you could."

He told me that one day the church would awaken to common goals. That causes would unite us. I knew He wasn't telling me everything, but I felt inspired by this thought, that things like missions had united us for centuries and this area of hopelessness in me for a united church was washed with hope for a God who is strong in our weaknesses. Arise, Lord and heal us. What a great world could we have if we united the church.

Part 4: There is Enough

God is not concerned about our differences as much as we seem to be. We've lost the humility that allows us to be weak in the strength of the Lord. Shame will never do that for us. We will never lower our heads into unity. It's not possible. More and more, God will swallow up our lack in "more than enough." "Death is swallowed up in victory."[30] A common ground for every one of us is that Christ won for all of us.

Our heads are bowed in humility to God, not in shame to each other. To each other, we learn to give. We learn to be a culture of generosity. We sow into each other. We know there will be a great harvest, but we do it because that's what our strengths are there to do. They are there to both be strong and to provide for one another. There is enough when we embrace that we have something valuable to give to each other and the opportunity that presents to all of us.

You see it's not that subjects like global warming are a lie. There's science that's for it and science that's against it. But we seem to act like there are only two sides. Either foreboding fear or apathetic jeering. The truth is that we have opportunities to meet needs together as a global society. This should be every Christians dream but somehow we let politics take over. The real cause of this polar rhetoric is that we no longer trust each other to be great. But we are great, because we are made in the image of God. God is not

---

[30] *1 Cor. 15:54b NKJV*

up there thinking, "Oops, there's too many of them! Heaven, there's too many humans. What will we do?!" No, He's been full of intentionality this entire time, giving Abraham a starry sky worth of sons and daughters, and we all know that the sky is even more abundant than Abe could have imagined today.

Jesus is coming back, no doubt about it, but not for a piece of garbage. He's coming back for a spotless bride.[31] That's a statement full of faith about our future identity. It let's us know that we are capable through the life of Christ and resources that God has provided to actually be spotless. To be spotless, to be abounding with beauty, so lovely that forever, there will be a marriage between us and our Lord. I realize not everyone will see this the way I do and I'm not asking for that agreement. I'm loving the Word of God as we all should and looking for hope and light in it.

Maybe you don't see it the same, but abundance is available through heavenly resources; abundance that doesn't destroy, but builds up. That to me is a hope of God's glory. I pray that all of us would have great hope. There is much to be torn down and I don't deny that, but what I see is that the greatness of God, when seen in the land of the living, removes my thoughts from need and worry.

The encounters that God has given me have thoroughly convinced me that God is abundant and so abundant that nothing

---

[31] *Eph. 5:27*

will lack. Nothing will be "not enough." God makes things like He is, and He is Holy and high above. Nothing is left low when it knows who He is. Not even the earth that groans for us to know this about us.

He's not high above distant, but high above, inviting everything to come up with Him. We are but dirt after all. It is His breath that animates us and gives life to every living creature. That in and of itself is a picture of great abundance, evidence right here beating in our chest. He is abundant and if He is abundant, then His creation is abundant and there is more than enough.

Prayer Activation

Take a moment with each of the following exercise questions, prayers and activities. Give yourself a minimum of 3-5 minutes to respond to each.

When you picture God and say, "I am grateful", what do you see, sense, or feel? Is it hard to say? Is it effortless and overflowing? Is there anything else going on? Write it down.

_____

_____

_____

Did you have any trouble seeing or experiencing gratitude? If so, ask God why. Say, "Lord God, why can't I feel grateful?" and write that down, whatever He tells you. If it's a past hurt, an expectation unfulfilled, a lie you're believing or anything else, ask the Lord if you need to forgive. Ask Him what the lie is and then ask Him the truth and write it down. Ask Him, who you need to forgive if it feels like that's the block. If it's a wall, ask Him if He wants to help you take it down. Ask Him to help you see the wall. What's the wall made out of? Ask Him if He has a tool to help you take it down with Him. Keep asking questions until your gratitude is overflowing in worship.

_____

_____

_____

Go back and do this exercise again as many times as you like. Try replacing the word "gratitude" with Kingdom of Heaven supplies like "joy, peace and righteousness." Remember these things don't originate in you. They come from heaven and that is how they are infinite and eternal. Grab all you can.

Try a prophetic act: As you discover your access and His supply imagine yourself putting your discoveries in a crown on your head. Lock it down in a jewels setting with a twist (act it out in faith as an exercise).

I once had an encounter where I would lift that crown up, look at it and then throw it back at Jesus' feet. He reached down picked it up and with the best smile I've ever seen and so much joy in His fiery eyes and He put it back on my head. I threw it down again and He picked it up and put it on my head again. We did this with increasing speed and rhythm until it became a rather violent but loving dance between us. With great big smiles and feet off the ground, we laughed and repeated over and over.

Take these exercises with you and use them anywhere in any way that you feel led by the Lord to do so. He is faithful to lead you. I am confident having known His love for myself that He passionately loves you and wants you to know all of Him without reservation.

Did you have an encounter during this exercise? Or do you want to read about other encounters that people have had? Visit our Facebook group to tell others about it and spread the good news. See Appendix A of this book for help writing or filming your testimony. I pray that you receive these encounter gifts abundantly. Please see Appendix A for more information.

Part 4: There is Enough

Thank You So Much for Joining Me

> *"Look at how much encouragement you've found in your relationship with the Anointed One! You are filled to overflowing with his comforting love. You have experienced a deepening friendship with the Holy Spirit and have felt his tender affection and mercy."* Philippians 2:1 TPT

Guys, I'm so grateful that you would take the time to read this manuscript that I believe the Lord gave me. You've truly made the process worth it. My hope is that it truly has allowed you to move deeper, higher and further than you could have ever imagined into the depths of His overwhelming grace and love.

I pray that you would be kept by Him, that angels would protect each and every moment you share together, and that you would walk in sound truth all the days ahead. That your relationship with God would heal your past, future and that the present would become the most exciting union with Him. Abundance would mark your days and your purpose and identity for all to see.

I pray that you wouldn't have to go anywhere without our Lord God's tangible presence! I pray He would lavishly reteach you all of life with Emanuel. I bless you as a son in His inheritance. I bless you with every blessing He has given me. May you greatly prosper all the way through your being in every single way to wholeness and overflow, and spend every day in the house of the Lord with Him.

May you be blessed with dreams, visions, gifts of healing, deliverance and so much more. I pray all the desires of that precious heart He gave you would come into full abundance. That your faith, hope and love would be defended, counseled and advocated for all the days of your life by heaven's greater counsel in the throne room of God.

I pray that you feel a strength from heaven to share your testimonies and get abundant opportunities. I pray that you would always know the best way to articulate it with the effortless support of the Holy Spirit, like the breath of life He is pouring out from your voice. I pray that your words would be the containers of Christ life on the earth today.

I pray that like the promise I received declared, that this book has effectively delivered to you the gift of encounters that He so generously gave to me. May you know Jesus, Holy Spirit and Father God like they know each other. May you become one, like Jesus wanted for you and I.

May you know the church and the abundance of God. May my ceiling be your floor and may you and I both know sustainable revival in the life of Christ here in the land of the living. May we supply the foundations for all the generations that will follow us. May we greatly please the Lord past His every expectation, so much that His song bursts forth over us, reshaping the earth into the heaven forever.

God, we give you all the glory. You are worthy to be praised in every moment of our eternal days. Please, forever and ever, teach us how, reshape us and mold us into the eternal image of Your precious Son, Jesus Christ.

Amen~

Appendix A
How to Tell Your Testimony

> *They conquered him completely through the blood of the Lamb and the powerful word of His testimony. They triumphed because they did not love and cling to their own lives, even when faced with death.*
>
> *Romans 12:11*

Share the Testimony

Hopefully, if you've picked this book up, you're beginning to understand the power of the testimony. It is the very thing that God will use through us to overcome. In 1 Corinthians 15:54b in the NKJV, it declares in all uppercase, "DEATH IS SWALLOWED UP IN VICTORY!" and the victory is what Christ has done through us.

This is the hope of glory for all of us. Our testimony swallows up death. It swallows up the power that death has held over us. Love cast out the fear of death, but our testimony gives us confidence, and a passionate fighting spirit to get in its face when the darkness is closing in. Our victory, which is His testimony in us, overcomes every kind of death and destruction, sickness, disease, hopelessness, and so on. We cannot underestimate the power of the testimony.

If you learn to tell your testimony, others will overcome by hearing what Christ has done for you. It might happen then and there, or it might be years from that moment, when they're in the

Appendix A: How to Tell Your Testimony

dark. Just then, the Holy Spirit brings it to memory that light has overcome this darkness before, and that this isn't a challenge for what Jesus can do.

There's even testimonies of this happening to people who died and went to hell. I vaguely recall a testimony of a man who died and in hell, he recalled his Sunday school teacher telling them to call on Jesus and sang a song to them. He couldn't remember Jesus' name for some time, but kept rehearsing the song until it came back to his memory. He declared that in the moment he said it, he was suddenly sucked out of hell and brought to a bright white room. Jesus stood before Him with the keys to hell in His hand. The man was given another chance to live and was revived after being dead for nearly half an hour or more. The testimony of Jesus from that song saved this man's life from hell!

It's likely that his Sunday school teacher had no idea the weight of their testimony to save this man. She probably thought she was just sharing a song, but her conviction about that song stuck with this man and the victory of Christ overcame death.

Your testimony could do the same and more.

Testimonies about our encounters with God, include how we hear, see, taste or and smell Him. I remember walking into a service once and smelling a powerful smell, like frankincense. Only I didn't know what frankincense smelled like until later in my life. It might have been subjective, but for me it was real. I was there, and it stuck out to me. Not all testimonies are life and death, but of course these little moments matter too. So many have been delivered from drugs, sadness, suicidal thoughts, even hell. Tell the big testimonies but tell the little ones too. The relational aspect of all of the moments are the encounter. Tell the encounter. Share the testimony!

Appendix A: How to Tell Your Testimony

Tips for Preparing the Testimony

The following may apply to most testimonies about inner healings, physical healing, words of knowledge confirmed and more. These are also tips for sharing well (expanded upon in the coming sections):

1. *Tell someone you trust your testimony before you share it with the world. I'm always surprised at what didn't make sense, or how people will connect more with a small aspect of my testimony that I didn't feel was the most important part until I heard them process it. Additionally, pay attention to how it feels. Is it dark or troublesome or is it life bringing? You'll know the difference easily.*
2. *Only say what you know is accurate. Only say what is currently verifiable. It needs to be loving and honoring towards all others and especially*

people, places, things that are mentioned in the testimony.

3. Mention previous medical help, if any, in the testimony. Honor the medical community. There's nothing second class about the healing that doctors do (paraphrasing Paul Manwaring there) but it is helpful to remember that not everyone knows where you've been. If you've been diagnosed previously and now there is a good medical report, the world needs to see the proof whenever possible. Grab the evidence and, if possible, provide the visuals.

4. Be specific with all the details you have, without "filling in the blanks" on any details you don't have. Keep it short, focused and refined (from 1 to 3-minute videos and 1 to 3 paragraph posts whenever possible).

5. Let the testimony speak for itself. You don't have to teach it. Jesus told parables and trusted the parable to contain everything that it needed for those that were supposed to hear it. We should do likewise. No need to push an agenda down anyone's throat. This generation seems very protective towards agenda. They seem to smell it before buying the movie ticket, in most cases. Trust the story and tell it like it happened. Let the story do the heavy lifting. The Holy Spirit knows

everyone. He knows how to reach them too. No need to try to do His work for Him.

6. *If you're talking about Jesus, then Jesus is getting the glory. No need to follow everything up with a religious sounding statement like, "Jesus is the only one. He did it all." Is that even true? Were you even there? Did doctors play a part? Jesus is not in a competition with you and if He really did it all and you weren't even a part of the good that happened, then wouldn't the whole thing have been even better? These are good questions to help get ourselves to be as real and authentic as possible. Jesus uses you and I to bless others. It's His power, but He gave it to us to use. Give Him honor, but don't do that at your expense. That's not right. You matter to Him and you should matter to you. If someone else thinks otherwise, it's their problem, not yours.*

In general, many follow these three steps as well when trying to convey helpful information to an audience of any size. It's simple and easy to remember. Let the delivery of your message:

1. *Say what you are going to say.*
2. *Say what you are saying.*

3. *Say what you said again.*

It won't work for every kind of testimony of course, but the core of this approach is that it will help the hearer hear. It will help the information to stick. The art of storytelling is a powerful help and it's easy to find classes online for free or at a small cost. Check out EdX online, where it's free to audit classes from great universities and others.

All I can say is, we should invest our time to give it our very best. We don't have to become a writer, but most of us can read a few blogs, take a writing class, or watch a few YouTubes in the interest of making our testimony more palatable. Go all out if you can. Give it your very best.

At the same time, don't give up on telling it because you don't have the time to make it perfect, or even good. If you don't have the time or energy to invest in making a big effort, give it what you can. Jesus commented on the women with two mites.[32] Give like she did regardless of your ability.

---

[32] *Luke 21:2*

Appendix A: How to Tell Your Testimony

Consider the Best Platform for Your Testimony

What is the best way to present your testimony? Should you write it out, video it, or prepare to give it as a sermon? Should you do all of these things? The Israelites would create ceremonies to celebrate their testimonies and help them remember it. Should you have a testimony birthday every year, or something like that? Should you share your testimony by writing and creating a Children's book!? Should you have a cartoon track in your back pocket about your testimony for when you're on the streets praying with people? Maybe all of the above?

Is it a song? An equipping book like this one? Should it be a screenplay? If so, how long? Feature length or is it a fifteen-minute filler kind of screenplay? Maybe it's a mini-series? Never in history have more screenplays been needed. Netflix and other streaming services are constantly under the pressure from consumers to produce new content. There is a good chance your screenplay can get picked up. Especially if it's excellent, verifiable and creative.

If you're not sure, you should practice it, rehearse it between you and the Holy Spirit. He will help you. Sometimes when I rehearse my testimonies, the Lord opens up a vision of the audience and everything.

I highly recommend writing it down. This isn't necessarily for the screen play. This is just to help you sort through the details. Do this as soon as possible. Journal it as long as it comes out, and then shorten it. Boil it down again and again. Boil it down. Boil all the water out until it's a nice soup of nutritious goodness with every single bite!

For example, this book is half the size it was when I first finished it. I was blessed to find an excellent editor who wasn't afraid to tell me that I could do better. She worked with me until I realized that even if everything I wrote down was meaty, it was still too much and needed to be sorted out. The book you have here is far more focused and direct. It feels like a sharpened sword compared to the other one.

If you started with a twenty-page version, boil it down to a ten page and then a five page and so on. Most of the testimonies I shared in this book have been written out five or more times. I've written Facebook post, blogs, and even this book a few times now. I've told them over and over and lost count as I keep them handy for any kind of ministry I'm doing. They are a part of my helmet of salvation, if you ask me.

If you're not the writing type, then video it. If the first time you video it, it's thirty minutes long, then boil that down into a ten minute version and get it down to a thirty second version. What are the key points? What are the things that you can leave to the hearer's imagination? When people have to work out some of the details, it leaves room for them to move from spectator into participant. Is that a good thing? If not, don't do it. In today's world, less is generally more. Say what you want to say in as few words as possible, for everyone's sake.

Accuracy and Specifics

Being able to speak out a powerful testimony requires a grounding in the Word of God and a commitment to authenticity. Keep it Holy and real! If you had a cool experience that no one would understand, and you can't find a Scripture to back it up, avoid putting something like that out there. No need to discount it as all bad, just don't share something you don't have peace about. Be blessed to be blessed and keep it to yourself.

Protect the truth with your whole heart of love and respect for Jesus and others. Do not violate your relationship with God! Put Him first. He will guide you with peace when you ask Him.

With that said, not everyone will understand, no matter how clear it is to you. Your good friends might get it sometimes and others, not. It's fine. A lot of the testimonies you read here in my book might show up much later in your life to give you hope. Testimonies work like that a lot. Give them anyway without putting pressure on yourself.

Never forsake authenticity. If you're not being real and telling it from your heart, maybe don't tell it. I love that this generation can't stomach plastic smiles and fakeness. Don't be fake. Don't feel like you have to be the teacher. The testimony carries glory with it. If received, then it can be perceived and even conceived as their own encounter at times. Give people permission to have your encounter and let God do it again.

The point of accuracy and specifics is not that you recount every tiny detail, either. The purpose of accuracy and specifics is that you don't leave out any of the important stuff. Although some of your testimony may be subjective, try to stick to verifiable information the best that you possibly can. Line up the dates on a timeline. Visit the places it happened again if it's been a while.

Obviously, there isn't a need to exaggerate. Even the small things God does are valuable. Keep in mind that if He did anything at all, His nature has been revealed. Again, no matter how small. If it's clear that God has a desire to heal something ten percent, it could help others to have faith for the remaining ninety percent. Just because it's not complete doesn't diminish the power of God to heal, but the faith you share can help others to believe for more. Be as excellent in your accuracy as possible.

Getting Permission

Get permission. Always get permission from the people you'll mention. But consider if places or things are mentioned in your testimony. Is there even a chance that the person you mention could disagree? If so, get permission. Never assume, it's just better for you if you don't. It's also more honoring to them. Don't get held down with a commitment to accuracy and specifics here. It's better to just call it a store, than to name the popular chain in most cases. There are exceptions, of course, and for that you'll need wisdom and the Holy Spirit.

Appendix A: How to Tell Your Testimony

Using Honor & Wisdom

Jesus is the reason for the testimony. Honor Jesus.

Testimonies aren't brags about where we've been and who we've met. If our life in Christ leads us to pray for a famous person, for example, then what we can talk about is how Christ can reach everyone. Maybe even mention that it was a famous person so long as people won't be able to make the connection. We have access to Holy Spirit wisdom. We should always run our testimonies by Him. Is there peace on our testimony? Maybe save it, if not. Sometimes He wants us to share the testimony,[33] but sometimes He does not[34]. He leads us to share with some people, but sometimes not with others. Let Him have these choices. It's a relationship.

---

[33] *Luke 8:39*

[34] *Mark 1:41-44*

How to Tell the Testimony

In the popular business book, *Building a Story Brand*, by Donald Miller,[35] we are given the traditional "seven elements of great story telling." Our testimony isn't a business speech, or sales strategy, but this book does a great job of helping us pull the pieces together to tell a vivid, engaging story. It just needs a few tweaks. Here is the general outline for how to tell a great story, according to Miller:

> "A CHARACTER who wants something encounters a PROBLEM before they can get it. At the peak of their despair, a GUIDE steps into their lives, gives them a PLAN, and CALLS THEM TO ACTION. That action helps them

---

[35] Miller, Donald. Building a Storybrand: Clarify Your Message so Customers Will Listen. HarperCollins Leadership, an Imprint of HarperCollins, 2017.

avoid FAILURE and ends in a SUCCESS." Donald Miller, Building a Storybrand-

Both Miller and I feel like this framework is applicable to many platforms, even the testimony. This structure for delivering your content is simply one of the easiest ways to keep the human attention span, especially in a day of information overload. Even Jesus' parables followed similar frameworks like this.

Consider my favorite parable, the Prodigal Son, and how the prodigal son is the character who has a problem, meets his father, the guide, and is invited into the house for a party, but first is given a ring and a robe to take authority with. That ring and robe are now his inheritance and with them his life will be both successful and he can avoid future failures. Like Miller points out, we see this in the best movies, books, marketing and so many more forms of communication. Let's take a look at how we can apply it to our testimonies.

CHARACTER and PROBLEM or OPPORTUNITY: While every testimony ultimately has to do with Jesus, your testimony of what Jesus can do will likely be how you—or anyone you are telling the testimony about—overcame with the help of Jesus as a GUIDE. To both clarify and help the listener to hear you, it can be helpful to point out how the character and problem or opportunity is also your audience, or relatable and relevant to something they have faced, or could face.

For example: "I faced a common dilemma," or "like many of us, I found myself in a place of great debt (or heartache, physical pain from... and so on)." On the OPPORTUNITY side, the testimony could be stating something like; "We all believe God for this and when I did believe Him, it opened my eyes to this opportunity..." or "We all have access to a generous Father and so when I grabbed onto that truth, *this* miracle/sign/wonder began to happen."

PLAN: In general, the plan presented by the Gospel (i.e. "I turned to Jesus and He healed me like He did others in the Gospels") is the PLAN I'm referring to. God has presented each of us a PLAN that is also an act of love and sacrifice that gives us access to our inheritance of empowerment to overcome, change, be healed, be restored, be renewed and so on.

That is our CALL TO ACTION, if you will. It is how "DEATH IS SWALLOWED UP IN VICTORY" as the NKJV says in 1 Corinthians 15:54b. It is the reason you're giving your testimony. This is the moment of HOPE that we all can do all things through Christ who strengthens us[36] or it is the moment of HOPE that we too can overcome an existing injustice. Your experience is evidence of God's LOVE on the earth through either FAITH we had or FAITH it gave us. Faith we had for something that came to pass or faith it gave us after something happened unexpectedly.

---

[36] *Paraphrase from Phil. 4:13*

Obviously, these aren't rules for telling the testimony, but rather helpful wineskins. You may have noticed that I deviated from this framework or have seen where someone else has and that is because the wine is the most important part when it comes to wineskins. This framework is like the wineskin, but the testimony is the wine. Let the wine take precedence and have value above the wineskin to the point that you can decide what wineskin to use that is best suited for your wine. For your testimony.

Who is your CHARACTER?

_____

_____

_____

What PROBLEM OR OPPORTUNIY did you or they face?

_____

_____

_____

How did a GUIDE help you/them? (i.e. Jesus, God, Holy Spirit, the Bible, Inheritance, Family of God or Church, Encounter with Heaven, and so on)

_____

_____

_____

What or how does the GUIDE give a PLAN and does that relate to what God is doing on the earth today? Where is the gospel message in this testimony? Where is Jesus revealed or the purpose of God's eternal plan for either me or all of us revealed?

_____

_____

_____

What is the ACTION that took place? How did the Character take a step, make an choice that the GUIDE recommended and so on? What was the moment of power from Holy Spirit? How did wisdom from the Bible present a change that brought about a victory? What can the listener do to either join in the celebration or make a change themselves?

_____

_____

_____

Appendix A: How to Tell Your Testimony

What is the victory like now? What is the HOPE that you can leave each of us with from this testimony and how it can change us or help us receive what God has for our future? Either our future as individuals or our future as a body?

_____

_____

_____

If you filled this out just now then *congratulations*! You have just placed your *testimony wine* into one of the most ancient, tried and true *wineskins* known to man! It's a format that well generally capture the attention of people and hold it. This process has been shaping stories for thousands of years. So hopefully it has really helped to make the very most out of your testimony. Not only that, but you finished it off with a powerful seed that could change lives and set individuals, nations, even the whole world free from what was faced. God uses the blood of the Lamb and the word of our testimony about Jesus to bring us all to overcome together in Jesus Christ!

Like to a magnet, people and even angels gather around us to hear our testimonies. Our media feeds, movies, and more are all waiting to hear this kind of hope rising up and delivering a dying world.

Let your heaven come, Lord God. We pray let it be on earth as it is in heaven. And we thank you Lord for overcoming the world with Your love and purposes. May our testimonies deliver all from bondage and suffering and into Your loving embrace forever. Amen.

Appendix A: How to Tell Your Testimony

Invitation

~

Do you have a testimony you want to share on our public Facebook group?! Visit our group to spread the good news of Jesus Christ. I believe that God wants to normalize the testimony lifestyle of encounters and overcoming daily!

If you'd like to share a testimony anonymously, please email testimonies@abundantencounters.com with all the needed permission and or direction and instructions (for example, if you wish that we not share your testimony, please tell us, otherwise we will remove your name and other specifics, so we can post them in a way that honors and keeps the testimony).

As I've said, the thought of having a public database of the supernatural activities of God thrills me to no end. Being that it is social media, you need to understand that you are posting publicly however and at your own risk. We, of course, cannot take responsibility for how your testimony will be received or shared. Please assume that everyone has access and will read it because that is possible. I again pray that you receive these encounter gifts abundantly.

Find this community on Facebook and share your testimony at: www.facebook.com/groups/abundantencounters/

Appendix B
365 Encounters Bible Reading Plan

Over the years designing this plan, I have been determined to be intentional about flow. Specifically, flow that would encourage me toward encounters. I don't believe you have to choose this plan to receive encounters. No, and even in all my efforts and thoughts about it, I only ever decided to create a plan that I loved personally. A plan that loved me. A plan that felt connected.

This plan has everything I love for a daily dive into OT, NT, Proverbs and ending with the passionate, emotional experience in the Psalms. It's important to both enter and exit my reading time with the Lord with passion. It's important to be intentional about our affections on a daily basis. It's usually 6am or so when I start, so I'm not the most passionate at that time, but my love isn't turned off as I move toward what many have called the greatest love letter ever written.

Nevertheless, flow has continually stood out to me as a sort of really important consideration for anyone learning to live in the

Word. Flow keeps us from getting stuck. If you're floating down a river and hit a wall something has stopped the flow. Adjustments need to be made. I recommend that as you read, you value flow. For example, be willing to sacrifice the genealogies if needed... the Holy Spirit will highlight them when He wants you to read them, or you'll get a little nudge to go back, etc. Just follow that flow. Don't worry about rules, instead long for the adventure and expect His face.

Have both a reading option and a listening option for when you don't feel like reading. It's so simple. The You Version Bible App that is free to smart phones is amazing for when you just want to keep up with your plan. It is never helpful to beat yourself up over what you've missed. Just find ways to get back into it. Don't waste your time with self-criticism during this effort. Make this a holy place, set apart from all condemnation.

Other important tips... Maybe try using accents or different voices for each Scriptural person, and character you come across on your reading. It's important to take the time to get to know the voices in your Scriptures. However you want to do that.

Try different translations! Gosh, I love *The Passion Translation, The Message, The New King James, The New American Standard, The Mirror Bible, The Amplified,* even *The Rhyming Gospel* (which is great to read to kids). There are so many.

At one point, I decided to read a different translation each year, but it was too hard to stay with one translation. In the course of the year, I found myself missing more familiar translations. If the

Word becomes words only, then try changing it up, and see if it resurrects. It's worth it, friends!

As I've said, this is not a good religious duty to maintain. It is a meal to enjoy with a loving Father. Rote religion and rules can try to replace the encounters with duty. Guard your heart from such suffering with all diligence.

Maybe even more important than flow is to set aside the time. In the book of Joshua Chapter 3:1, 6:12, 7:16 and 8:10 it says again and again in each verse, Josh woke early in the morning. So, I wake early in the morning. Simple ☺

Be aware. If you have not made the time and the space for something new to exist in your life, you will not likely maintain your discipline. Be realistic when it comes to this kind of thing and set aside the time. Consider setting aside a unique space if possible. A place where you won't be tempted to do other things. A focus spot.

The easiest way to do this has always been for me to set aside the first fruits of my morning time for the Lord. It's just His and He can do whatever He wants with it. I do it first and early, because if I don't, before I can blink, here comes something to steal it away. I'd also recommend those early hours because it is the quietest, most serene time of the entire day.

And finally, always give yourself more time than you need. The encounters may come any time during the day or night, but this time is set aside to eat and drink in the Word. It's a valuable transaction that I believe God has completely designed us to make with great ease to our heart at a small cost. We win big in this. Keep it up for forty days and they say it will be habit.

If you can, find a way to print the following pages. Make the declarations each day, add some journal time to your schedule as well. It's all for connection. The veil is gone between you and the Father, so go to Him now. Sit with Him and hear Him read to you with your heart and your mind.

All the very best to you,

Josh-

Appendix B: 365 Encounters Bible Reading Plan

JANUARY DAY	OT	NT	Proverbs	Psalms
1	Gen. Introduction	Matt. 1:1-2:12	Prov. 1:1-7	Ps. 1
2	Gen. 1	Matt. 2:13-3:17	Prov. 1:8-13	Ps. 2:1-6
3	Gen. 2	Matt. 4	Prov. 1:14-19	Ps. 2:7-12
4	Gen. 3	Matt. 5:1-26	Prov. 1:20-23	Ps. 3
5	Gen. 4	Matt. 5:27-48	Prov. 1:24-28	Ps. 4
6	Gen. 5	Matt. 6:1-24	Prov. 1:29-33	Ps. 5:1-6
7	Gen. 6	Matt 6:25-7:14	Prov. 2:1-5	Ps. 5:7-12
8	Gen. 7	Matt. 7:15-29	Prov. 2:6-15	Ps. 6:1-5
9	Gen. 8	Matt. 8:1-22	Prov. 2:16-22	Ps. 6:6-10
10	Gen. 9	Matt. 8:23-34	Prov. 3:1-4	Ps. 7:1-5
11	Gen. 10	Matt. 9:1-17	Prov. 3:5-8	Ps. 7:6-10
12	Gen. 11	Matt. 9:18-38	Prov. 3:9-10	Ps. 7:11-17
13	Job Introduction	Matt. 10:1-16	Prov. 3:11-12	Ps. 8:1-4
14	Job 1,2	Matt. 10:17-42	Prov. 3:13-15	Ps. 8:5-9
15	Job 3,4	Matt. 11	Prov. 3:16-18	Ps. 9:1-6
16	Job 5,6	Matt. 12:1-21	Prov. 3:19-20	Ps.9:7-12
17	Job 7,8	Matt. 12:22-50	Prov. 3:21-26	Ps. 9:13-16
18	Job 9,10	Matt. 13:1-23	Prov. 3:27-32	Ps. 9:17-20
19	Job 11,12	Matt. 13:24-46	Prov. 3:33-35	Ps. 10:1-6
20	Job 13,14	Matt. 13:47-14:12	Prov. 4:1-6	Ps. 10:7-13
21	Job 15,16	Matt. 14:13-36	Prov. 4:7-9	Ps. 10:14-18
22	Job 17,18	Matt. 15:1-28	Prov. 4:10-13	Ps. 11
23	Job 19,20	Matt. 15:29-16:12	Prov.4:14-19	Ps. 12
24	Job 21,22	Matt. 16:13-28	Prov. 4:20-27	Ps. 13
25	Job 23,24	Matt. 17	Prov. 5:1-6	Ps. 14
26	Job 25,26	Matt. 18:1-20	Prov. 5:7-14	Ps. 15
27	Job 27,28	Matt. 18:21-19:12	Prov. 5:15-21	Ps. 16:1-5
28	Job 29,30	Matt. 19:13-30	Prov. 5:22-23	Ps. 16:6-11
29	Job 31,32	Matt. 20:1-28	Prov. 6:1-5	Ps. 17:1-7
30	Job 33,34	Matt. 20:29-21:22	Prov. 6:6-11	Ps. 17:8-15
31	Job 35,36	Matt. 21:23-46	Prov. 6:12-15	Ps. 18:1-6

ENCOUNTERS ~ Pressing into Your Abundant Heavenly Supply ~

FEBRUARY DAY	OT	NT	Proverbs	Psalms
1	Job 37,38	Matt. 22:1-33	Prov. 6:16-19	Ps. 18:7-16
2	Job 39,40	Matt. 22:34-23:12	Prov. 6:20-23	Ps. 18:17-24
3	Job 41	Matt. 23:13-39	Prov. 6:24-35	Ps. 18:25-31
4	Job 42	Matt. 24:1-28	Prov. 7:1-5	Ps. 18:32-38
5	Gen. 12,13	Matt. 24:29-51	Prov. 7:6-23	Ps. 18:39-45
6	Gen. 14,15	Matt. 25:1-30	Prov. 7:24-27	Ps. 18:46-50
7	Gen. 16,17	Matt. 25:31-26:13	Prov. 8:1-11	Ps. 19:1-6
8	Gen. 18,19	Matt. 26:14-46	Prov. 8:12-13	Ps. 19:7-14
9	Gen. 20,21	Matt. 26:47-68	Prov. 8:14-21	Ps. 20
10	Gen. 22,23	Matt. 26:69-27:10	Prov. 8:22-31	Ps. 21:1-7
11	Gen. 24	Matt. 27:11-32	Prov. 8:32-36	Ps. 21:8-13
12	Gen. 25,26	Matt. 27:33-66	Prov. 9:1-6	Ps. 22:1-5
13	Gen. 27	Matt. 28:1-20	Prov. 9:7-8	Ps. 22:6-11
14	Gen. 28-30	Mark Introduction & 1:1-28	Prov. 9:9-10	Ps. 22:12-19
15	Gen. 31	Mark 1:29-2:12	Prov. 9:11-12	Ps. 22:20-24
16	Gen. 32,33	Mark 2:13-3:6	Prov. 9:13-18	Ps. 22:25-31
17	Gen. 34,35	Mark 3:7-30	Prov. 10:1-2	Ps. 23
18	Gen. 36,37	Mark 3:31-4:25	Prov. 10:3-4	Ps. 24:1-6
19	Gen. 38-40	Mark 4:26-5:20	Prov. 10:5	Ps. 24:7-10
20	Gen. 41	Mark 5:21-43	Prov. 10:6-7	Ps. 25:1-7
21	Gen. 42	Mark 6:1-29	Prov. 10:8-9	Ps. 25:8-14
22	Gen. 43,44	Mark 6:30-56	Prov. 10:10	Ps. 25:15-22
23	Gen. 45,46	Mark 7:1-23	Prov. 10:11-12	Ps. 26:1-7
24	Gen. 47,48	Mark 7:24-8:10	Prov. 10:13-14	Ps. 26:8-12
25	Gen. 49,50	Mark 8:11-38	Prov. 10:15-16	Ps. 27:1-6
26	Exodus Introduction	Mark 9:1-29	Prov. 10:17	Ps. 27:7-14
27	Ex. 1,2	Mark 9:30-10:12	Prov. 10:18	Ps. 28
28	Ex. 3,4	Mark 10:13-31	Prov. 10:19	Ps. 29:1-5
29	Ex. 5,6	Mark 10:32-52	Prov. 10:20-21	Ps. 29:6-11

Appendix B: 365 Encounters Bible Reading Plan

MARCH DAY	OT	NT	Proverbs	Psalms
1	Ex. 7,8	Mark 11:1-26	Prov. 10:22	Ps. 30:1-5
2	Ex. 9,10	Mark 11:27-12:17	Prov. 10:23	Ps. 30:6-12
3	Ex. 11,12	Mark 12:18-37	Prov. 10:24-25	Ps. 31:1-6
4	Ex. 13,14	Mark 12:38-13:13	Prov. 10:26	Ps. 31:7-14
5	Ex.15,16	Mark 13:14-37	Prov. 10:27-28	Ps. 31:15-19
6	Ex. 17,18	Mark 14:1-21	Prov. 10:29-30	Ps. 31:20-24
7	Ex. 19,20	Mark 14:22-52	Prov. 10:31-32	Ps. 32:1-5
8	Ex. 21,22	Mark 14:53-72	Prov. 11:1-3	Ps. 32:6-11
9	Ex. 23,24	Mark 15:1-20	Prov. 11:4	Ps. 33:1-7
10	Ex. 25,26	Mark 15:21-47	Prov. 11:5-6	Ps. 33:8-15
11	Ex. 27,28	Mark 16:1-20	Prov. 11:7	Ps. 33:16-22
12	Ex. 29,30	Luke 1:1-25	Prov. 11:8	Ps. 34:1-7
13	Ex. 31,32	Luke 1:26-56	Prov. 11:9-11	Ps. 34:8-14
14	Ex. 33,34	Luke 1:57-80	Prov. 11:12-13	Ps. 34:15-22
15	Ex. 35,36	Luke 2:1-20	Prov. 11:14	Ps. 35:1-10
16	Ex. 37,38	Luke 2:21-52	Prov. 11:15	Ps. 35:11-18
17	Ex. 39,40	Luke 3	Prov. 11:16-17	Ps. 35:19-23
18	Leviticus Intro. & Ch. 1	Luke 4:1-30	Prov. 11:18-19	Ps. 35:24-28
19	Lev. 2-4	Luke 4:31-5:11	Prov. 11:20-21	Ps. 36:1-6
20	Lev. 5-7	Luke 5:12-32	Prov. 11:22	Ps. 36:7-12
21	Lev. 8-10	Luke 5:33-6:11	Prov. 11:23	Ps. 37:1-6
22	Lev. 11,12	Luke 6:12-36	Prov. 11:24-26	Ps. 37:7-13
23	Lev. 13	Luke 6:37-7:10	Prov. 11:27	Ps. 37:14-19
24	Lev. 14, 15	Luke 7:11-35	Prov. 11:28	Ps. 37:20-27
25	Lev. 16,17	Luke 7:36-8:3	Prov. 11:29-31	Ps. 37:28-33
26	Lev. 18,19	Luke 8:4-21	Prov. 12:1	Ps. 37:34-40
27	Lev. 20-22	Luke 8:22-39	Prov. 12:2-3	Ps. 38:1-9
28	Lev. 23-25	Luke 8:40-9:6	Prov. 12:4	Ps. 38:10-15
29	Lev. 26-27	Luke 9:7-27	Prov. 12:5-7	Ps. 38:16-22
30	Numbers Intro. a& Ch. 1	Luke 9:28-50	Prov. 12:8-9	Ps. 39:1-5
31	Num. 2-4	Luke 9:51-10:12	Prov. 12:10	Ps. 39:6-11

ENCOUNTERS ~ *Pressing into Your Abundant Heavenly Supply* ~

APRIL DAY	OT	NT	Proverbs	Psalms
1	Num. 5,6	Luke 10:13-37	Prov. 12:11-12	Ps. 39:12-13
2	Num. 7	Luke 10:38-11:13	Prov. 12:13-15	Ps. 40:1-7
3	Num. 8-10	Luke 11:14-36	Prov. 12:16-17	Ps. 40:8-13
4	Num. 11-13	Luke 11:37-12:12	Prov. 12:18	Ps. 40:14-17
5	Num. 14-16	Luke 12:13-34	Prov. 12:19-20	Ps. 41:1-4
6	Num. 17-19	Luke 12:35-59	Prov. 12:21-23	Ps. 41:5-13
7	Num. 20-22	Luke 13:1-21	Prov. 12:24	Ps. 42:1-5
8	Num. 23-25	Luke 13:22-14:6	Prov. 12:25	Ps. 42:6-11
9	Num. 26-28	Luke 14:7-35	Prov. 12:26	Ps. 43
10	Num. 29-31	Luke 15	Prov. 12:27-28	Ps. 44:1-8
11	Num. 32-34	Luke 16:1-18	Prov. 13:1	Ps. 44:9-17
12	Num. 35-36	Luke 16:19-17:10	Prov. 13:2-3	Ps. 44:18-22
13	Deut. Intro. & Ch 1	Luke 17:11-37	Prov. 13:4	Ps. 44:23-26
14	Deut. 2-4	Luke 18:1-17	Prov. 13:5-6	Ps. 45:1-8
15	Deut. 5-7	Luke 18:18-19:10	Prov. 13:7-8	Ps. 45:9-17
16	Deut. 8-10	Luke 19:11-40	Prov. 13:9-10	Ps. 46:1-7
17	Deut. 11-13	Luke 19:41-20:8	Prov. 13:11	Ps. 46:8-11
18	Deut. 14-16	Luke 20:9-26	Prov. 13:12-14	Ps. 47:1-4
19	Deut. 17-19	Luke 20:27-47	Prov. 13:15-16	Ps. 47:5-9
20	Deut. 20,21	Luke 21:1-28	Prov. 13:17-19	Ps. 48:1-8
21	Deut. 22,23	Luke 21:29-22:13	Prov. 13:20-23	Ps. 48:9-14
22	Deut. 24,25	Luke 22:14-38	Prov. 13:24-25	Ps. 49:1-7
23	Deut. 26,27	Luke 22:39-53	Prov. 14:1-2	Ps. 49:8-13
24	Deut. 28	Luke 22:54-23:12	Prov. 14:3-4	Ps. 49:14-20
25	Deut. 29-31	Luke 23:13-43	Prov. 14:5-6	Ps. 50:1-6
26	Deut. 32-34	Luke 23:44-24:12	Prov. 14:7-8	Ps. 50:7-14
27	Joshua Intro. & ch 1	Luke 24:13-53	Prov. 14:9-10	Ps. 50:15-23
28	Josh. 2-4	John 1:1-28	Prov 14:11-12	Ps. 51:1-6
29	Josh. 5-7	John 1:29-51	Prov. 14:13-14	Ps. 51:7-11
30	Josh. 8-10	John 2	Prov. 14:15-16	Ps. 51:12-19

Appendix B: 365 Encounters Bible Reading Plan

MAY DAY	OT	NT	Proverbs	Psalms
1	Josh. 11-13	John 3:1-21	Prov. 14:17-19	Ps. 52
2	Josh. 14-16	John 3:22-36	Prov. 14:20-21	Ps. 53
3	Josh. 17-19	John 4:1-30	Prov. 14:22-24	Ps. 54
4	Josh. 20-22	John 4:31-54	Prov. 14:25	Ps. 55:1-7
5	Josh. 23-24	John 5:1-24	Prov. 14:26-27	Ps. 55:8-14
6	Judg. Intro. & Ch 1	John 5:25-47	Prov. 14:28-29	Ps. 55:15-19
7	Judg. 2-4	John 6:1-21	Prov. 14:30-31	Ps. 55:20-23
8	Judg. 5-7	John 6:22-42	Prov 14:32-33	Ps. 56:1-7
9	Judg. 8-10	John 6:43-71	Prov. 14:34-35	Ps. 56:8-13
10	Judg. 11-13	John 7:1-36	Prov. 15:1-3	Ps. 57:1-6
11	Judg. 14-16	John 7:37-53	Prov. 15:4	Ps. 57:7-11
12	Judg. 17-19	John 8:1-20	Prov. 15:5-7	Ps. 58:1-6
13	Judg. 20-21	John 8:21-30	Prov. 15:8-10	Ps. 58:7-11
14	Ruth Intro. & Ch 1	John 8:31-59	Prov. 15:11-12	Ps. 59:1-5
15	Ruth 2-4	John 9	Prov. 15:13-14	Ps. 59:6-13
16	1Sam. Introduction	John 10:1-21	Prov. 15:15-17	Ps. 59:14-17
17	1Sam 1,2	John 10:22-42	Prov. 15:18-19	Ps. 60:1-4
18	1Sam 3,4	John 11:1-30	Prov. 15:20-21	Ps. 60:5-12
19	1Sam 5,6	John 11:31-57	Prov. 15:22-23	Ps. 61
20	1Sam 7,8	John 12:1-19	Prov. 15:24-26	Ps. 62:1-8
21	1Sam 9,10	John 12:20-50	Prov. 15:27-28	Ps. 62:9-12
22	1Sam 11,12	John 13:1-30	Prov. 15:29-30	Ps. 63:1-5
23	1Sam 13,14	John 13:31-14:14	Prov. 15:31-32	Ps. 63:6-11
24	1Sam 15,16	John 14:15-31	Prov. 15:33	Ps. 64:1-6
25	1Sam 17,18	John 15	Prov. 16:1-3	Ps. 64:7-10
26	1Sam19,20	John 16	Prov. 16:4-5	Ps. 65:1-7
27	1Sam 21,22	John 17	Prov. 16:6-7	Ps. 65:8-13
28	1Sam 23,24	John 18:1-24	Prov. 16:8-9	Ps. 66:1-7
29	1Sam 25,26	John 18:25:25-19:16	Prov. 16:10-11	Ps. 66:8-15
30	1Sam 27,28	John 19:17-42	Prov. 16:12-13	Ps. 66:16-20
31	1Sam 29,30	John 20	Prov. 16:14-15	Ps. 67

ENCOUNTERS ~ *Pressing into Your Abundant Heavenly Supply* ~

JUNE DAY	OT	NT	Proverbs	Psalms
1	1Sam 31, 1Cron 10	John 21	Prov. 16:16-17	Ps. 68:1-7
2	2Sam Introduction	Acts 1	Prov. 16:18	Ps. 68:8-19
3	2Sam 1,2	Acts 2:1-36)	Prov. 16:19-20	Ps. 68:20-26
4	2Sam 3,4	Acts 2:37-3:26	Prov. 16:21-23	Ps. 68:27-35
5	1Cron. Introduction	Acts 4	Prov.16:24	Ps. 69:1-6
6	1Cron 1,2	Acts 5	Prov. 16:25	Ps. 69:7-13
7	1Cron 3,4	Acts 6	Prov.16:26-27	Ps. 69:14-18
8	1Cron 5,6	Acts 7:1-29	Prov. 16:28-30	Ps. 69:19-25
9	1Cron 7,8	Acts 7:30-53	Prov. 16:31-33	Ps. 69:26-30
10	1Cron 9, 2Sam 5:1-10	Acts 7:54-8:24	Prov. 17:1	Ps. 69:31-36
11	1Cron 11,12	Acts 8:25-40	Prov. 17:2-3	Ps. 70
12	2Sam 5:11-6:23	Acts 9:1-25	Prov. 17:4-5	Ps. 71:1-7
13	1Cron 13,14	Acts 9:26-43	Prov. 17:6	Ps. 71:8-17
14	1Cron 15,16	Acts 10:1-23	Prov. 17:7-8	Ps. 71:18-24
15	2Sam 7, 1Cron 17	Acts 10:24-48	Prov. 17:9-11	Ps. 72:1-7
16	2Sam 8,9	Acts 11	Prov. 17:12-13	Ps. 72:8-14
17	1Cron 18, 2Sam 10	Acts 12	Prov. 17:14-15	Ps. 72:15-20
18	1Cron 19, 2Sam 11	Acts 13:1-23	Prov. 17:16	Ps. 73:1-5
19	2Sam 12, 1Cron 20	Acts 13:24-41	Prov. 17:17-18	Ps. 73:6-12
20	2Sam 13,14	Acts 13:42-14:7	Prov. 17:19-21	Ps. 73:13-18
21	2Sam 15-17	Acts 14:8-28	Prov. 17:22	Ps. 73:19-23
22	2Sam 18,19	Acts 15:1-35	Prov. 17:23	Ps. 73:24-28
23	2Sam 20,21	Acts 15:36-16:15	Prov. 17:24-25	Ps. 74:1-9
24	2Sam 22-23:7	Acts 16:16-40	Prov. 17:26	Ps. 74:10-17
25	2Sam 23:8-39	Acts 17	Prov. 17:27-28	Ps. 74:18-23
26	2Sam 24, 1Cron 21	Acts 18:1-23	Prov. 18:1	Ps. 75:1-3
27	1Cron 22,23	Acts 18:24-19:10	Prov. 18:2-3	Ps. 75:4-10
28	1Cron 24,25	Acts 19:11-41	Prov. 18:4-5	Ps. 76:1-3
29	1Cron 26,27	Acts 20	Prov. 18:6-7	Ps. 76:4-9
30	1Cron 28,29	Act 21:1-14	Prov. 18:8	Ps. 76:10-12

Appendix B: 365 Encounters Bible Reading Plan

JULY DAY	OT	NT	Proverbs	Psalms
1	1King Intro. & Ch. 1	Acts 21:15-34	Prov. 18:9-10	Ps. 77:1-9
2	1King 2	Acts 21:35-22:22	Prov. 18:11-12	Ps. 77:10-15
3	1King 3, 4	Acts 22:23-23:11	Prov. 18:13	Ps. 77:16-20
4	2Cron. Intro. & Ch. 1	Acts 23:12-35	Prov. 18:14-15	Ps. 78:1-7
5	1King 5,6	Acts 24	Prov. 18:16-18	Ps. 78:8-12
6	2Cron 2,3	Acts 25	Prov. 18:19	Ps. 78:13-20
7	1King 7, 2Cron 4	Acts 26	Prov. 18:20-21	Ps. 78:21-29
8	1King 8, 2Cron 5	Acts 27:1-20	Prov. 18:22	Ps. 78:30-35
9	2Cron 6,7	Acts 27:21-44	Prov. 18:23-24	Ps. 78:36-42
10	1King 9, 2Cron 8	Acts 28	Prov. 19:1-3	Ps. 78:43-51
11	Eccles. Intro. & Ch. 1	Song. 1-2	Prov. 19:4-5	Ps. 78:52-58
12	Ecc. 2-4	Song. 3-4	Prov. 19:6-7	Ps. 78:59-64
13	Ecc. 5-8	Song. 5-6	Prov. 19:8-9	Ps. 78:65-72
14	Ecc. 9-12	Song. 7-8	Prov. 19:10-12	Ps. 79:1-8
15	1King 10, 11	Rom. 1:1-17	Prov. 19:13-14	Ps. 79:9-13
16	1King 12, 2Cron 9	Rom. 1:18-32	Prov. 19:15-16	Ps. 80:1-6
17	1King 13, 14	Rom. 2	Prov. 19:17	Ps. 80:7-11
18	2Cron 10,11 & 1King 15:1-24	Rom. 3:1-20	Prov. 19:18-19	Ps. 80:12-19
19	2Cron 12, 13	Rom. 3:21-31	Prov. 19:20-21	Ps. 81:1-7
20	2Cron 14, 15	Rom. 4	Prov. 19:22-23	Ps. 81:8-16
21	2Cron 16, 1King 15:25-16:34	Rom. 5	Prov. 19:24-25	Ps. 82
22	2Cron 17, 1King 17	Rom. 6	Prov. 19:26-27	Ps. 83:1-8
23	1King 18,19	Rom. 7	Prov. 19:28-29	Ps. 83:9-18
24	1King 20,21	Rom. 8:1-13	Prov. 20:1	Ps. 84:1-8
25	1King 22, 2Cron 18	Rom. 8:14-30	Prov. 20:2-3	Ps. 84:9-12
26	2Cron 19,20	Rom. 8:31-9:9	Prov. 20:4-6	Ps. 85:1-2
27	2Cron 21-23	Rom. 9:10-33	Prov. 20:7	Ps. 85:3-13
28	Obadiah Intro. & Ch. 1	Rom. 10	Prov. 20:8-10	Ps. 86:1-10
29	2King Intro. &Ch. 1	Rom. 11:1-15	Prov. 20:11	Ps. 86:11-17
30	2King 2,3	Rom. 11:16-36	Prov. 20:12	Ps. 87
31	2King 4,5	Rom. 12	Prov. 20:13-15	Ps. 88:1-7

ENCOUNTERS ~ Pressing into Your Abundant Heavenly Supply ~

AUGUST DAY	OT	NT	Proverbs	Psalms
1	2King 6,7	Rom. 13	Prov. 20:16-18	Ps. 88:8-13
2	2King 8,9	Rom. 14	Prov. 20:19	Ps. 88:14-18
3	2King 10,11	Rom. 15:1-21	Prov. 20:20-21	Ps. 89:1-4
4	2King 12,13	Rom. 15:22-33	Prov. 20:22-23	Ps. 89:5-11
5	2Cron 24	Rom. 16:1-27	Prov. 20:24-25	Ps. 89:12-18
6	2King 14, 2Cron 25	1Cor. 1:1-17	Prov. 20:26-27	Ps. 89:19-26
7	Jonah Intro. & Ch. 1	1Cor. 1:18-2:5	Prov. 20:28-30	Ps. 89:27-37
8	Jonah 2-4	1Cor. 2:6-16	Prov. 21:1-2	Ps. 89:38-45
9	2King 15, 2Cron26	1Cor. 3	Prov. 21:3	Ps. 89:46-52
10	Isaiah Intro. & Ch 1	1Cor. 4	Prov. 21:4	Ps. 90:1-8
11	Is. 2-4	1Cor. 5	Prov. 21:5-7	Ps. 90:9-17
12	Is. 5-8	1Cor. 6	Prov. 21:8-10	Ps. 91:1-8
13	Amos Intro. & Ch 1	1Cor. 7:1-24	Prov. 21:11-12	Ps. 91:9-16
14	Amos 2-4	1Cor. 7:25-40	Prov. 21:13	Ps. 92:1-7
15	Amos 5,6	1Cor. 8	Prov. 21:14-16	Ps. 92:8-15
16	Amos 7,8	1Cor. 9:1-18	Prov. 21:17-18	Ps. 93
17	Amos 9, 2Cron 27	1Cor. 9:19-10:12	Prov. 21:19-20	Ps. 94:1-8
18	Is. 9,10	1Cor. 10:13-33	Prov. 21:21-22	Ps. 94:9-15
19	Is. 11,12	1Cor. 11:1-16	Prov. 21:23-24	Ps. 94:16-23
20	Micah Intro. & Ch. 1	1Cor. 11:17-34	Prov. 21:25-26	Ps. 95:1-5
21	Micah 2-4	1Cor. 12:1-26	Prov. 21:27	Ps. 95:6-11
22	Micah 5-7	1Cor. 12:27-13:13	Prov. 21:28-29	Ps. 96:1-6
23	2Cron 28, 2King 16	1Cor. 14:1-19	Prov. 21:30-31	Ps. 96:7-13
24	2King 17, Is. 13	1Cor. 14:20-40	Prov. 22:1	Ps. 97:1-6
25	Is. 14,15	1Cor. 15:1-28	Prov. 22:2-4	Ps. 97:7-12
26	Is. 16-18	1Cor. 15:29-58	Prov. 22:5-6	Ps. 98
27	Is. 19-21	1Cor. 16	Prov. 22:7	Ps. 99
28	Is. 22-24	2Cor. 1:1-14	Prov. 22:8-9	Ps. 100
29	Is. 25-27	2Cor. 1:15-2:13	Prov. 22:10-12	Ps. 101
30	2King 18:1-8, 2Cron 29	2Cor. 2:14-3:6	Prov. 22:13	Ps. 102:1-7
31	2Cron 30,31	2Cor. 3:7-18	Prov. 22:14	Ps. 102:8-14

Appendix B: 365 Encounters Bible Reading Plan

SEPTEMBER DAY	OT	NT	Proverbs	Psalms
1	Hosea Intro. & Ch. 1	2Cor. 4	Prov. 22:15	Ps. 102:15-21
2	Hosea 2-4	2Cor. 5:1-10	Prov. 22:16	Ps. 102:22-28
3	Hosea 5-7	2Cor. 5:11-21	Prov. 22:17-19	Ps. 103:1-7
4	Hosea 8-10	2Cor. 6:1-13	Prov. 22:20-21	Ps. 103:8-13
5	Hosea 11-14	2Cor. 6:14-7:7	Prov. 22:22-23	Ps. 103:14-22
6	Is. 28-30	2Cor. 7:8-16	Prov. 22:24-25	Ps. 104:1-7
7	Is. 31-33	2Cor. 8:1-15	Prov. 22:26-27	Ps. 104:8-14
8	Is. 34-35	2Cor. 8:16-24	Prov. 22:28-29	Ps. 104:15-22
9	2King 18,19	2Cor. 9	Prov. 23:1-3	Ps. 104:23-29
10	2King 20,21	2Cor. 10	Prov. 23:4-5	Ps. 104:30-35
11	Is. 36-38	2Cor. 11:1-15	Prov. 23:6-8	Ps. 105:1-7
12	Is. 39-41	2Cor. 11:16-33	Prov. 23:9-11	Ps. 105:8-15
13	Is. 42-44	2Cor. 12:1-10	Prov. 23:12	Ps. 105:16-22
14	Is. 45-47	2Cor. 12:11-21	Prov. 23:13-14	Ps. 105:23-30
15	Is. 48-50	2Cor. 13	Prov. 23:15-16	Ps. 105:31-37
16	Is. 51-53	Gal. 1	Prov. 23:17-18	Ps. 105:38-45
17	Is. 54-56	Gal. 2:1-14	Prov. 23:19-21	Ps. 106:1-6
18	Is. 57-59	Gal. 2:15-3:14	Prov. 23:22	Ps. 106:7-14
19	Is. 60,61	Gal. 3:15-29	Prov. 23:23	Ps. 106:15-22
20	Is. 62,63	Gal. 4	Prov. 23:24	Ps. 106:23-28
21	Is. 64-66	Gal. 5:1-15	Prov. 23:25-28	Ps. 106:29-35
22	2Cron 32,33	Gal. 5:16-26	Prov. 23:29-35	Ps. 106:36-43
23	Nahum Intro. & Ch. 1	Gal. 6	Prov. 24:1-2	Ps. 106:44-48
24	Nahum 2,3	Eph. 1	Prov. 24:3-4	Ps. 107:1-8
25	2King 22,23	Eph. 2	Prov. 24:5-6	Ps. 107:9-16
26	2Cron 34,35	Eph. 3	Prov. 24:7	Ps. 107:17-24
27	Zeph Intro. & Ch. 1	Eph. 4:1-16	Prov. 24:8	Ps. 107:25-32
28	Zeph 2,3	Eph. 4:17-32	Prov. 24:9-10	Ps. 107:33-38
29	Jer. Intro. & Ch. 1	Eph. 5	Prov. 24:11-12	Ps. 107:39-43
30	Jer 2,3	Eph. 6	Prov. 24:13-14	Ps. 108:1-6

ENCOUNTERS ~ Pressing into Your Abundant Heavenly Supply ~

OCTOBER DAY	OT	NT	Proverbs	Psalms
1	Jer 4,5	Phil. 1	Prov. 24:15-16	Ps. 108:7-13
2	Jer 6,7	Phil. 2:1-18	Prov. 24:17-20	Ps. 109:1-8
3	Jer 8,9	Phil. 2:19-3:4	Prov. 24:21-22	Ps. 109:9-15
4	Jer 10,11	Phil. 3:5-21	Prov. 24:23-25	Ps. 109:16-21
5	Jer 12,13	Phil. 4	Prov. 24:26	Ps. 109:22-26
6	Jer 14,15	Col. 1:1-14	Prov. 24:27	Ps. 109:27-31
7	Jer 16,17	Col. 1:15-2:5	Prov. 24:28-29	Ps. 110
8	Jer 18,19	Col. 2:6-23	Prov. 24:30-34	Ps. 111
9	Jer 20,21	Col. 3:1-17	Prov. 25:1-5	Ps. 112
10	Jer 22,23	Col. 3:18-4:18	Prov. 25:6-8	Ps. 113
11	Jer 24,25	1Thess. 1:1-2:12	Prov. 25:9-10	Ps. 114
12	Jer 26,27	1Thess. 2:13-3:13	Prov. 25:11-14	Ps. 115:1-8
13	Jer 28,29	1Thess. 4	Prov. 25:15	Ps. 115:9-18
14	Jer 30,31	1Thess. 5	Prov. 25:16	Ps. 116:1-9
15	Jer 32,33	2Thess. 1	Prov. 25:17	Ps. 116:10-19
16	Jer 34,35	2Thess. 2	Prov. 25:18-19	Ps. 117
17	Jer 36,37	2Thess. 3	Prov. 25:20-22	Ps. 118:1-7
18	Jer 38,39	1Tim. 1	Prov. 25:23-24	Ps. 118:8-14
19	2King 24,25	1Tim. 2	Prov. 25:25-27	Ps. 118:15-21
20	2Cron 36	1Tim. 3	Prov. 25:28	Ps. 118:22-29
21	Haba. Intro. & Ch. 1	1Tim. 4	Prov. 26:1-2	Ps. 119:1-8
22	Haba. 2,3	1Tim. 5	Prov. 26:3-5	Ps. 119:9-16
23	Jer 40-42	1Tim. 6	Prov. 26:6-8	Ps. 119:17-24
24	Jer 43-45	2Tim. 1	Prov. 26:9-12	Ps. 119:25-32
25	Jer 46-48	2Tim. 2	Prov. 26:13-16	Ps. 119:33-40
26	Jer 49,50	2Tim. 3	Prov. 26:17	Ps. 119:41-48
27	Jer 51	2Tim. 4	Prov. 26:18-19	Ps. 119:49-56
28	Jer 52	Titus 1	Prov. 26:20	Ps. 119:57-64
29	Lam. Intro. & Ch. 1	Titus 2	Prov. 26:21-22	Ps. 119:65-72
30	Lam. 2,3	Titus 3	Prov. 26:23	Ps. 119:73-80
31	Lam. 4,5	Philem. 1-25	Prov. 26:24-26	Ps. 119:81-88

Appendix B: 365 Encounters Bible Reading Plan

NOVEMBER DAY	OT	NT	Proverbs	Psalms
1	Ezek. Intro. & Ch. 1	Heb. 1	Prov. 26:27	Ps. 119:89-96
2	Ezek 2-4	Heb. 2	Prov. 26:28	Ps. 119:97-104
3	Ezek 5,6	Heb. 3	Prov. 27:1-2	Ps. 119:105-112
4	Ezek 7,8	Heb. 4	Prov. 27:3	Ps. 119:113-120
5	Ezek 9,10	Heb. 5	Prov. 27:4-6	Ps. 119:121-128
6	Ezek 11,12	Heb. 6	Prov. 27:7-9	Ps. 119:129-136
7	Ezek 13-15	Heb. 7:1-12	Prov. 27:10	Ps. 119:137-144
8	Ezek 16	Heb. 7:13-28	Prov. 27:11	Ps. 119:145-152
9	Ezek 17,18	Heb. 8	Prov. 27:12	Ps. 119:153-160
10	Ezek 19,20	Heb. 9:1-10	Prov. 27:13	Ps. 119:161-168
11	Ezek 21,22	Heb. 9:11-28	Prov. 27:14	Ps. 119:169-176
12	Ezek 23,24	Heb. 10:1-18	Prov. 27:15-16	Ps. 120
13	Ezek 25,26	Heb. 10:19-39	Prov. 27:17	Ps. 121
14	Ezek 27,28	Heb. 11:1-16	Prov. 27:18-20	Ps. 122
15	Ezek 29,30	Heb. 11:17-31	Prov. 27:21-22	Ps. 123
16	Ezek 31,32	Heb. 11:32-12:17	Prov. 27:23-27	Ps. 124
17	Ezek 33,34	Heb. 12:18-29	Prov. 28:1	Ps. 125
18	Ezek 35,36	Heb. 13	Prov. 28:2	Ps. 126
19	Ezek 37,38	James 1	Prov. 28:3-5	Ps. 127
20	Ezek 39,40	James 2	Prov. 28:6-7	Ps. 128
21	Ezek 41,42	James 3	Prov. 28:8-10	Ps. 129
22	Ezek 43,44	James 4	Prov. 28:11	Ps. 130
23	Ezek 45,46	James 5	Prov. 28:12-13	Ps. 131
24	Ezek 47,48	1Peter 1:1-12	Prov. 28:14	Ps. 132:1-7
25	Joel Intro. & Ch. 1	1Peter 1:13-2:10	Prov. 28:15-16	Ps. 132:8-12
26	Joel 2,3	1Peter 2:11-3:7	Prov. 28:17-18	Ps. 132:13-18
27	Dan. Intro. & Ch. 1	1Peter 3:8-4:6	Prov. 28:19-20	Ps. 133
28	Dan. 2	1Peter 4:7-5:14	Prov. 28:21-22	Ps. 134
29	Dan. 3,4	2Peter 1	Prov. 28:23-24	Ps. 135:1-7
30	Dan. 5,6	2Peter 2	Prov. 28:25-26	Ps. 135:8-14

ENCOUNTERS ~ *Pressing into Your Abundant Heavenly Supply* ~

DECEMBER DAY	OT	NT	Proverbs	Psalms
1	Dan. 7,8	2 Peter 3	Prov. 28:27-28	Ps. 135:15-21
2	Dan. 9,10	1John 1	Prov. 29:1	Ps. 136:1-7
3	Dan. 11,12	1John 2:1-17	Prov. 29:2-4	Ps. 136:8-14
4	Ezra Intro. & Ch. 1	1John 2:18-3:3	Prov. 29:5-7	Ps. 136:15-21
5	Ezra 2,3	1John 3:4-24	Prov. 29:8-11	Ps. 136:22-26
6	Ezra 4-6	1John 4	Prov. 29:12-14	Ps. 137
7	Haggai Intro.	1John 5	Prov. 29:15-17	Ps. 138
8	Hag. 1-2	2John, 3John	Prov. 29:18	Ps. 139:1-7
9	Zac. Intro. & Ch. 1	Jude 1-25	Prov. 29:19-20	Ps. 139:8-16
10	Zac. 2-4	Rev. 1	Prov. 29:21-22	Ps. 139:17-24
11	Zac. 5-7	Rev. 2:1-17	Prov. 29:23	Ps. 140:1-5
12	Zac. 8-10	Rev. 2:18-3:6	Prov. 29:24-25	Ps. 140:6-13
13	Zac. 11-13	Rev. 3:7-22	Prov. 29:26-27	Ps. 141:1-4
14	Esther Intro.	Rev. 4	Prov. 30:1-3	Ps. 141:5-10
15	Esther 1,2	Rev. 5	Prov. 30:4	Ps. 142
16	Esther 3,4	Rev. 6	Prov. 30:5-8	Ps. 143:1-6
17	Esther 5,6	Rev. 7	Prov. 30:9-10	Ps. 143:7-12
18	Esther 7,8	Rev. 8	Prov. 30:11-14	Ps. 144:1-6
19	Esther 9,10	Rev. 9	Prov. 30:15-16	Ps. 144:7-15
20	Ezra 7,8	Rev. 10	Prov. 30:17	Ps. 145:1-7
21	Ezra 9,10	Rev. 11	Prov. 30:18-20	Ps. 145:8-14
22	Neh. Intro. & Ch. 1	Rev. 12	Prov. 30:21-23	Ps. 145:15-21
23	Neh. 2,3	Rev. 13	Prov. 30:24-28	Ps. 146:1-5
24	Neh. 4,5	Rev. 14	Prov. 30:29-31	Ps. 146:6-10
25	Lam. 3:37-5:22	Rev. 15-16	Prov. 30:32	Ps. 147:1-7
26	Neh. 6,7	Rev. 17	Prov. 30:33	Ps. 147:8-14
27	Neh. 8,9	Rev. 18	Prov. 31:1-3	Ps. 147:15-20
28	Neh. 10,11	Rev. 19	Prov. 31:4-7	Ps. 148:1-7
29	Neh. 12,13	Rev. 20	Prov. 31:8-9	Ps. 148:8-14
30	Malachi Intro. & Ch. 1	Rev. 21	Prov. 31:10-24	Ps. 149:1-9
31	Mal. 2-4	Rev. 22	Prov. 31:25-31	Ps. 150:1-6

Book References

THE LOVE DARE © Kendrick S, Kendrick A, Kimbrough L. Nashville, Tenn. : B & H Publishing Group, c2013.; 2013. ISBN: 9781433679599

THE KNOWLEDGE OF THE HEART © 2012 by Phil Mason. All rights reserved. ISBN: 9781621660705 New Earth Tribe Publications © 2012. U.S.A. Edition. Published by XP Publishing, a department of XP Ministries. www.XPpublishing.com

THE CONVERSATION IN HEAVEN: Living Life's Ups & Downs Through Heaven's Lens ©2018 Abigail Holt Jennings www.girlofhope.com all rights reserved. ISBN: 1727396111

TRIBAL LEADERSHIP: Leveraging Natural Groups to Build a Thriving Organization. Logan, D., King, J. P., & Fischer-Wright, H. (2011). New York : Harper Business, 2011, ©2008. ISBN: 9780061251320

Bible References

Du Toit, Francois. Mirror Bible. Hermanus, South Africa : Mirror Word Publishing, [2012], 2012.

Scripture quotations marked TPT are from The Passion Translation®. Copyright © 2017, 2018 by Passion & Fire Ministries, Inc. Used by permission. All rights reserved. www.ThePassionTranslation.com.

Scripture taken from the New King James Version®. Copyright © 1982 by Thomas Nelson. Used by permission. All rights reserved.

Scripture quotations taken from the Amplified® Bible (AMPC), Copyright © 1954, 1958, 1962, 1964, 1965, 1987 by The Lockman Foundation. Used by permission. www.Lockman.org

Scripture quotations taken from the New American Standard Bible® (NASB), Copyright © 1960, 1962, 1963, 1968, 1971, 1972, 1973, 1975, 1977, 1995 by The Lockman Foundation. Used by permission. www.Lockman.org

Scripture quotations marked (NIV) are taken from the Holy Bible, New International Version®, NIV®. Copyright © 1973, 1978, 1984, 2011 by Biblica, Inc.™ Used by permission of Zondervan. All rights reserved worldwide. www.zondervan.com The "NIV" and "New International Version" are trademarks registered in the United States Patent and Trademark Office by Biblica, Inc.™

Scripture quotations are from the ESV® Bible (The Holy Bible, English Standard Version®), copyright © 2001 by Crossway, a publishing ministry of Good News Publishers. Used by permission. All rights reserved.

www.ingramcontent.com/pod-product-compliance
Lightning Source LLC
Chambersburg PA
CBHW020403080526
44584CB00014B/1159